D1553363

Woman in Front of the Sun

Woman in Front of the Sun

ON BECOMING A WRITER

Judith Ortiz Cofer

THE UNIVERSITY OF GEORGIA PRESS

ATHENS & LONDON

Published by the University of Georgia Press
Athens, Georgia 30602
© 2000 by Judith Ortiz Cofer
Designed by Erin Kirk New
Set in 10/16 Fairfield by G & S Typesetters
Printed and bound by Thomson-Shore
The paper in this book meets the guidelines for
permanence and durability of the Committee on
Production Guidelines for Book Longevity of the
Council on Library Resources.

Printed in the United States of America

04 03 02 01 00 C 5 4 3 2 1
04 03 02 01 00 P 5 4 3 2 1

Library of Congress Cataloging-in-Publication Data
Ortiz Cofer, Judith, 1952–
Woman in front of the sun : on becoming a writer /
Judith Ortiz Cofer.
p. cm.
ISBN 0-8203-2261-x (alk. paper)
ISBN 0-8203-2242-3 (pbk.: alk. paper)
1. Ortiz Cofer, Judith, 1952– 2. Authors, American—
20th century—Biography. 3. Hispanic American
women—Biography. 4. Hispanic Americans—
Authorship. 5. Women—Authorship. 6. Authorship.
I. Title.
PS3565.R7737 Z478 2000
818'.5409—dc21
[B]
00-036882

British Library Cataloging-in-Publication Data available

To my mother and my daughter,

and to the other patient weavers who never give up

Spiders are patient weavers.

They never give up.

What keeps them at it?

Hunger, no doubt,

And hope.

—*May Sarton, "Love"*

CONTENTS

ACKNOWLEDGMENTS

Grateful acknowledgment is made to the following magazines and books in which the works in this book appeared, sometimes in slightly different versions:

"My Rosetta": First published in *Prairie Schooner* 74, no. 2 (summer 2000). Reprinted by permission of the University of Nebraska Press. Copyright 2000 University of Nebraska Press.

"A Prayer, a Candle, and a Notebook": First published as "Rituals: A Prayer, a Candle, and a Notebook" in *Becoming American: Personal Essays by First Generation Immigrant Women,* edited by Meri Nana-Ama Danquah (New York: Hyperion, 2000).

"The Gift of a *Cuento*": First published in *Las Christmas: Favorite Latino Authors Share Their Holiday Memories,* edited by

Esmeralda Santiago and Joie Davidow (New York: Alfred A. Knopf, 1998).

"Woman in Front of the Sun": First published in *New Letters* 65, no. 4 (1999).

"Before the Storm": First published in *El Coro: A Chorus of Latino and Latina Poetry,* edited by Martin Espada (Amherst: University of Massachusetts Press, 1995). Reprinted in *New Letters* 65, no. 4 (1999) as part of the essay "Woman in Front of the Sun."

"Taking the Macho": First published in *Prairie Schooner* 68, no. 4 (winter 1994). Reprinted by permission of the University of Nebraska Press.

"The Woman Who Slept with One Eye Open": First published in *The American Voice* 32 (fall 1993).

"The Woman Who Was Left at the Altar": First published in *Prairie Schooner* 59, no. 1 (spring 1985). Reprinted in *Reaching for the Mainland and Selected New Poems* by Judith Ortiz Cofer (Tempe, AZ: The Bilingual Press, 1995). Reprinted by permission of the University of Nebraska Press and the Bilingual Press.

Acknowledgments

"In Search of My Mentors' Gardens": First published in *Arts and Letters* (spring 2000).

"And Are You a Latina Writer?": Published in *The Americas Review,* guest editor Virgil Suarez, 24, nos. 3–4 (fall/winter 1996), and in *Máscaras,* edited by Lucha Corpi (Berkeley: Third Woman Press, 1997). Reprinted with permission from the publisher of *The Americas Review* 24, nos. 3–4 (Houston: Arte Publico Press—University of Houston, 1998).

"Claims": First published in *Prairie Schooner* 59, no. 1 (spring 1985). Reprinted by permission of the University of Nebraska Press.

"And May He Be Bilingual": First published in *Women/Writing/Teaching,* edited by Jan Zlotnik Schmidt (Albany: State University of New York Press, 1998). Copyright 1998 State University of New York Press.

"Latin Women Pray": First published in *New Mexico Humanities Review* 4, no. 1 (1981). Reprinted in *Reaching for the Mainland and Selected New Poems* by Judith Ortiz Cofer (Tempe, AZ: The Bilingual Press, 1995). Reprinted by permission of Bilingual Press.

Acknowledgments

"To Understand *El Azul*": First published in *Columns.*

I want to thank Karen Orchard for caring about this book from concept to production and my wonderful editor, Courtney Denney, for all the hours she put into the project; thanks also to Brad Edwards and Dan Shaw for their close readings of the manuscript, and the other friends whose insights helped me to shape this book.

Woman in Front of the Sun

My Rosetta

Sister Rosetta came into my life in 1966, at exactly the right moment. I was fourteen, beginning to stretch my bones after the long sleep of childhood, and the whole nation seemed to be waking up along with me. Each day the transistor radio I took everywhere informed me that the streets were alive with rebellion. Rock and roll filled the airwaves with throbbing sounds like those the heart makes when you are young and still listening to it—sounds that made me want to dance, yell, break out of my parents' cocoon of an apartment, sprout wings, and fly away from my predictable life and (what I feared most) a predictable future as a good Catholic barrio woman. Instead I was signed up for classes leading to my confirmation in the Catholic Church, spiritual preparation for the bishop's symbolic slap in the face: turn the other cheek, girl, you are now one of us humble followers of Christ. But my teacher in the ways of Christian humility, Sister Rosetta, was anything but the docile bride of Jesus I had expected.

She was not an attractive woman. Her face, although bright with wit, belonged on an Irish guy with a tough job, perhaps a construction foreman or a cop. If a nun's coif had not framed those features—the slightly bulbous nose, plump red-veined cheeks, and close-set eyes—this could have been the face of a heavy drinker or a laborer. She walked without grace but with a self-assured step we could hear approaching on the hardwood floors of the church basement where our lessons were held after school on cold winter afternoons in Paterson, New Jersey. Her rosary swinging from side to side on her habit's skirts, she strode in and slammed on the desktop whatever she was carrying that day. Then she'd lift herself onto the desk and face us, hands on hips as if to say, *What a shit job this is.*

And it was. Common knowledge had it that Sister Rosetta was assigned all the routine work of the convent by the Mother Superior to keep her busy and out of trouble. There was a rumor among us public school kids that Sister Rosetta had been arrested for taking part in a civil rights demonstration. And that she had been sent to our mainly Puerto Rican parish so that Father Jones, our saintly missionary pastor, could keep her under his wing. We found it funny to think of the shy, skinny man standing up to Sister Rosetta.

"OK, my little dumplings," Sister Rosetta would greet us, squinting like a coach about to motivate her team. "Today we are going to get in touch with our souls through music. Now listen carefully. You've never heard anything like this." Out of curiosity at first, then in near rapture, that day I listened to the exotic music of Ravi Shankar emerge from the old turntable Sister Rosetta had dragged in. The celestial notes of his sitar enveloped me in a gauzy veil of sound, stirring me in a new way. Sister had tacked the album cover on the corkboard, and as I looked deeply into Shankar's onyx eyes he seemed to look back: in his gaze there were answers to questions I was almost ready to ask.

She must have noticed my enchantment, because Sister Rosetta handed me that record album as I was walking out of her overheated classroom. All she said was, "Bring it back without a scratch." Much to my mother's annoyance, I played Shankar's music every day after school in my room while I did my homework. She called it *los gatos peleando,* the cat-fight album; but to me the high, lingering notes were an alarm clock bringing me out of myself, out of ignorance and into the realm

3

of the senses. For my thirteenth birthday I had received my own turntable and a Felipe Rodriguez album of Puerto Rican *boleros,* the romantic ballads my parents danced to at parties. I played the record occasionally for their sake, but Rodriguez's deep-throated laments about lost loves and weak women in tears did not appeal much to me. I liked the leaping, acrobatic images that Shankar's music induced, replacing my childhood dreams of flight.

In the guise of teaching Catholic doctrine, Sister Rosetta managed to introduce each of her classes to an eclectic curriculum that included folk music, Eastern philosophy, classical music, dance and yoga, world literary masterpieces, and popular culture. I watched in awe as this stocky, plain woman transformed herself into the most attractive person I knew whenever she talked with passionate eloquence about things all the other adults either ignored or disdained.

One day I was reading a book I had picked up in a restaurant booth. It was well worn, the front cover torn off as if someone had intended to hide his choice of reading material, and I had slipped it into my coat pocket before my parents noticed. The

4

word "lust," which appeared several times on the back cover blurbs, had enticed me to read the first chapter. Then the story had caught me in its sensational web: sex and sin described in clinical detail, right there in sentences and paragraphs just like the ones in my schoolbooks; characters who used drugs for fun; women who gained power through seduction.

This was a whole world I had only glimpsed in previews for movies when my father would take my mother and me to the theater that showed Spanish language films during the slow time on Sunday afternoons. I looked forward to these little forbidden clips that even in their brevity were more revealing than the Mexican or Argentinean films we watched, films with their predictable Cinderella themes of poor but talented (and, most important of all, *virtuous*) young women rescued from poverty, or from the danger of falling into a life of sin, by rich, handsome men—after, of course, having surmounted many obstacles to their love. The characters were almost always great dancers and singers, and a Mariachi band usually popped out from behind props to serenade the lovers at the appropriate moment. My parents held hands during the double feature, rapt in their escape into the fantasy. *May as well take what you can get,* I'd remind myself as I ate my popcorn, all the while making up in my head my own versions of the movies I did not get to see.

The book I had in my hands that day in Sister Rosetta's classroom, where I had arrived early to do my secret reading in solitude, had taken me into a dark, fascinating realm. Here were forbidden acts described in ordinary prose, no sermonizing about hells with boiling rivers of blood awaiting the sinners to be found in between the lines. Here was sanitized debauchery. Here was a world where drugs, sex, and fashion were all expensive pastimes. I knew about drug addiction from the news and neighborhood gossip, but the people shown there were either poor and dirty or exotic: hippies, gypsies, ghetto dwellers, and runaways, the lost people of our barrio who were the *drogadictos* our parents warned us about often. But in this book, drug use was exciting and glamorous. The women's clothes were described in the same intensely detailed manner as the rush they got from the pills and the diverse sex.

Transported out of my body by the text, I did not hear Sister Rosetta come in. She plucked the book out of my hands and, to my dismay, began reading aloud. In her no-nonsense voice, with that New Jersey accent, the drug-and-seduction scene sounded preposterous.

When Sister Rosetta slammed the book down on my desk, I kept my eyes lowered in shame. After a few moments, however, I was tricked by her silence into looking up, expecting an explosion of angry words. Instead I saw Sister Rosetta trying hard not to laugh aloud.

"Girlie," she said, still chuckling as she went over and closed the door (it was still ten minutes until class time), "why are you reading this trash?" She didn't wait for an answer. "Because it's there. Right? And as far as trash goes, this is pretty interesting." She let out her characteristic loud whistle to indicate that she was impressed. "Tell me, does reading this make you feel good or does it just tickle your fancy?"

Although baffled by her question, I was grateful that she had not reprimanded me, and I tried to think of an answer. I did feel excited about the things described in the book, of course, but I couldn't confess these feelings to Sister Rosetta or to anyone for that matter. I hadn't gone to confession for weeks because I could not bring myself to tell the priest about my dirty thoughts. Every day I risked dying without the sacraments, my soul blackened by mortal sin.

"I enjoy reading this book, Sister."

"I can see why. You want to know things your parents or I

7

will not teach you, and this book tells you about them—in glorious detail!" She laughed again. Then she sat on her desk and looked closely at me. "Honey, I can tell you have a hungry mind. Don't feed it junk. You wanna read about sex? It's mankind's favorite subject, from the Bible to *Fanny Hill*. People just can't stop writing about it. Next time you come, I'll have a few good books with plenty of sex in them for you. But these books weren't written by some glamour-puss for the money. They're art."

My face was burning. I couldn't believe that a nun, even the radical Sister Rosetta, was talking about sex so openly and offering to bring me books on the subject. For a minute I thought she was testing me, waiting for me to apologize and do penance. But students were now milling outside the door, and Sister Rosetta just said, "I'll keep this," dropping the book deep into one of her habit's bottomless pockets.

The next week she handed me a paper sack containing *Women in Love, Madame Bovary,* and *Wuthering Heights.* They were public library copies; she had actually checked out two books that I thought might be included in the church's list of banned writings! All she said was, "Make sure you put them in the drop box by the due date."

8

Of course I went home and lost myself in them. D. H. Lawrence appealed to me most, with his reckless immersion into language. Flaubert was too careful and precise for my taste. (I did not yet suspect that I had begun to read a page for the effect the words had on me rather than just for the juicy parts.) But it was the storm surging within Heathcliff that transported my imagination to places I wasn't yet quite able to identify.

Sister Rosetta continued to feed me books, neither asking me what I wanted nor quizzing me on their considerable effects. Under her tutelage, I read Hawthorne, Poe, *The Odyssey,* the stories of Katherine Anne Porter, Dante, the Romantic poets, even James Joyce (whose *Ulysses* was totally impenetrable, so I gave up on it). And always there was D. H. Lawrence, my dark, mysterious man, and the Brontës, who, like me, lived on the small planet of circumstance and who spoke to me about boundaries and how a smart woman might take flight through art. All the words I did not yet possess were my source of secret torment and joy. Sister Rosetta's was a reading list without apparent order, but it all came together inside me. My vocabulary expanded, my English improved, my restlessness doubled.

From these books I learned about desire and passion, but

also how to *think* about strong emotions. In grammar school I had once read a story about a boy who wanted muscles. An old man promises to teach him how to build his body in exchange for the boy's help with chores and errands. Day after day the boy chops wood, rakes the yard, paints the place, and does endless physical tasks for his mentor. Finally, many weeks later, the boy approaches the old man about keeping his end of the bargain. "It is time," the boy tells him. "I have done everything you have asked me to do: now teach me how to build muscles." Instead of answering, the old man leads the boy to a mirror. "Flex your arm," he says. And to the boy's amazement there are muscles in his arms.

I too was getting stronger without knowing it. I had begun to develop the inner eye that I needed to really see my life in the barrio and to look beyond it toward what I wanted from life. Why did the women around me complain about their lives of solitude and servitude but not take action? The only answer I got: *Así es la vida, Niña.* That's the way it is, our lives, your life, *la vida.* But why couldn't I go into church with my head uncovered as men did? Why did I have to advertise my sexual status by the color of the *mantilla* I was told to wear: white for *señoritas* and black for married women? That seemed a silly custom to me. Did God really care about such minutiae, or was this simply another male prerogative, to be able to identify which women were still available and which were already someone else's property? When I asked, however, I was told that my question was *impertinente,* and that I was a *malcriada,* an ill-mannered child and an embarrassment to my parents. This was a word always spoken in a sort of angry hiss during family arguments, a word that implied I was risking more than I could fathom.

But there were too many illogical rules, especially for girls and women, that were simply followed by mothers and taught to daughters: do not interrupt or join men's conversations; serve men first at meals; and, more infuriating to me than anything else, I was told that all boys (including my brother) needed to be outside more and more as they got older in order to "experience" the world. Girls, however, needed to stay home more each year because the world became more dangerous for a female as she matured.

As the walls of our apartment were closing in on me, I became determined to break out from what I saw as a suffocating cycle of acceptance and adherence to tradition. In my adolescent anger I failed to see that my dark fantasy of flight from everything my Puerto Rican family and neighbors stood for was in large part a normal stage of rebellion in the special setting of the barrio. There was so much there that I already loved: the sense of security that it gave my parents, the familiarity that was an oasis from *la lucha* whenever they came back from the alien culture of the American city to this Spanish-speaking island where favors were the currency most valued and the rules of the game were familiar. You do for me, I do for you; *mi casa es su casa,* and remember, *Compadre/Comadre,* when we are away from our *patria,* we are all *compañeros. ¿Verdad?* But even then I perceived that there was a suspension of reality involved. To play out the barrio-as-island fantasy, everyone had to agree not to question the rules.

My rebellion began at this delicate juncture: I wanted, needed, to learn how to see things for what they were before I could understand who I was in my more complex double world of school and home. The image I had in mind for myself was split: aligned with Joan Baez when I was feeling lyrical, but fiercely with Angela Davis when I seethed with the self-righteous fury of my struggle for autonomy. I wanted to break free, but first I had to have the right tools and a map for my great escape. Rosetta showed me how to get my hands on them.

A week before the bishop was due at our church to say confirmation mass, Sister Rosetta burst into our classroom with the layers of her skirts held high by huge safety pins, her muscular calves in thick, white cotton stockings displayed before our startled eyes. She had always worn the sleeves of the voluminous habit rolled back to her elbows, but this new alteration to the traditional medieval costume of the Sisters of Charity made her an outrageous sight to behold. I had never seen a nun's ankles, much less her legs. Without referring to her curious appearance, she taught the lesson for the day—a strange one if we were being programmed for humility. She talked about Christ's "righteous anger" at the money changers in the temple, how He had rebelled against an evil practice although it had been accepted in His time as tradition. As I took in Sister's every word, adding new ones to my vocabulary of rebellion, I felt my own chest filling up with the breath of Joan of Arc leading her soldiers to a holy battle. Rebellion.

"What is tradition?" she challenged, facing us in her military at-ease stance—eyes narrowed to slits.

After a long silence, I raised my hand: "Tradition is something that has always been done," I said.

"Like what, Judith?" With eyebrows raised nearly to her headgear, Sister Rosetta pushed me to state my position.

"Like wearing only certain types of clothes?" I cautiously ventured.

She smiled ironically at me, the eyebrows moving toward each other. "That is almost correct. Tradition is doing something because it has always been done. Sometimes this is good. It preserves culture, gives us tried-and-true ways to do things. But is it always good to do something in a particular way only because it has always been done that way?" She didn't wait for an answer this time: "No! Slavery was around for centuries; should we have kept that system? The guillotine is a quaint tradition. How about child labor?"

She rose to her full power as an orator that day. We looked at one another in amazement as Sister Rosetta listed horrors that at one time or another had been defended as tradition. Prejudice, cruelty to others, wars started with "traditional" enemies—it was a revelation to me to think from this new perspective, the beginning of hope for an argument against my parents' ways. Sister Rosetta's verbal rampage sparked the thought in my mind that it was possible to break free from a cycle. I began to understand the special power of words, the excitement that an image can generate.

Out of breath and her face flushed a bright red, Sister Rosetta concluded the day's class with a reading from Thoreau's "Civil Disobedience." Emboldened, I raised my hand again: "Is the idea of tradition sometimes used as an excuse for not changing things that need to be changed?" Her face relaxed, not quite into a smile but something better. What I had said was not yet my own thought. I had a good memory for quotes even then— a skill I later found useful for making impassioned speeches to my baffled relatives and as the lone Latina English student at college trying to impress her teachers. But leaders like to be quoted, and Sister Rosetta "noticed" me as a separate being in her captive motley crew of an audience.

Sister Rosetta's speech to us had been a rehearsal for a campaign she planned to initiate during the bishop's visit to our parish. Apparently she had been in correspondence with other progressive nuns around the country. They had started a petition to modify the nun's traditional vestments so as to bring the

Sisters of Charity into the twentieth century by liberating their limbs from the primitive shackles of cloth and heavy crosses, even as regular women were freeing their bodies from the modern harnesses of bras and girdles (at least the ones under the dreaded age of thirty). I was behind Sister Rosetta one hundred percent. On our last day of class she brought in a box of "Hello My Name Is" stickers on which was printed, VOTE BLUE! in bold marker script. She asked us to wear them on our choir robes the day of confirmation. As it turned out, only a few of us did, since most of the other kids in my class thought that Sister Rosetta had gone too far this time and that the bishop's visit was the wrong time for politics.

On confirmation day, I wore my VOTE BLUE! sticker proudly over my heart, pinned to my red and white choir robe. Did I imagine this, or did the bishop's hard eyes fall on the message right before he gave me my ceremonial slap? My cheek was still stinging when my mother came up to kiss me. Tears were in her eyes and also in mine, but for different reasons. Sister Rosetta's campaign was ultimately successful, since reform was in the air then—"the times they were a-changing" even in the church.

The caravan of cars she led to wherever nuns go to vote came back blowing horns in victory, and though many of the older sisters chose to keep their dangerous, bulky habits, the younger ones, the strong, new Sisters of Charity, walked with new freedom in reasonably lightweight, slate-blue outfits that did not come in the one-size-fits-all pattern of the old days.

That was doubtless a memorable triumph for Sister Rosetta. Though she may never know it, I regard myself as another of her triumphs. What I remember about the year I spent under this remarkable woman's tutelage is her teaching me to see with my whole self, not just with my eyes. Thanks to her, I learned that the power of knowledge lies in seeking the answer to the question I can always ask of the past, the present, and the future: *why?* Even now I can recall that summer, call up almost any memory in living color and in stereophonic sound, thanks to Sister Rosetta's training of my mind and her education of my senses. Her awareness-raising seminars were ridiculed by other nuns and laughed at by her more conservative students, but they gave me my first essential tool as a writer: the ability to absorb sensory detail from the pungent aroma of *la vida,* the siren call of religion, the sweet aftertaste of hard-won victory. I learned to re-experience it all at will in my mind and later on the page. Those months were the beginning of my long affair with the word, or should I say my lifetime commitment to it? The seductive power of language was introduced into my life when I needed it the most by the most unlikely and remarkable of my mentors, my radical sister, my Rosetta.

A Prayer, a Candle, and a Notebook

A Childhood Prayer

In the early days of my Spanish-language years
I was put under the care
of *El Angel de la Guarda,*
my Guardian Angel, the military sentinel
who required a nightly salute, a plea
on my knees for protection
against the dangers hidden in dreams,
and from night-prowling demons.

In the print framed over my bed,
he was portrayed as feathered and androgynous,
hovering above two barefoot children
whose features were set in pastel innocence—
crossing a dilapidated wood bridge

under which yawned a sulfurous abyss—
their only light being
the glow of the presence with wings
who was invisible to them.

I could take no comfort in this dark
nursery myth, as some nights
I lay awake listening to the murmur
of their voices sharing
their dreams of flight
in a well-lit kitchen, while I brooded
over the cruel indifference of adults
who abandoned children to the night,

and about that *Comandante* in the sky
who knew everything I did, or thought of doing,
whose minion could so calmly smile
while innocent children crossed over darkness,
alone, afraid, night after night.

Twice a month I talk on the telephone with my mother, who
lives in Puerto Rico. Today, after our usual exchange of news
about people on the Island whom I barely remember and
people in my life she has never met, I try to concentrate on

writing in my notebook. But Spanish has entered my brain, un-locking memories, making me take one of my trips back to my childhood in New Jersey and our first years in this country. I get my notebook from my dresser and settle down on the couch next to my textbooks and papers, which represent my real life now as an English professor at a southern university. At a safe distance from the chaotic world I grew up in—and Tennessee Williams was right when he said that "time is the longest dis-tance"—I now have enough space between my selves for my investigation to proceed. And that is why I write. I write to know myself, and it is a job that will occupy me for life.

Keeping track of my thoughts in a journal is a habit I ac-quired as a teenager experiencing the conflicts and loneli-ness of Puerto Rican immigrant life in the sixties. Now in my middle forties, I find writing my daily paragraph or two has be-come a routine as indispensable as a daily prayer and weekly candles are for my mother. Most nights before bed, I take out my plain school notebook and write a few lines. Every morning at dawn, I write the poems or begin the stories that my recol-lections have filtered through my dreams. I do not, however, merely record the mundane activities of each day in my journal or in my writings, but rather I try to capture with clarity and succinctness what, if anything, the past twenty-four hours have taught me. Sometimes as I write, my fingers cease to be connected to my conscious mind and instead become instruments of revelations of my most painful memories and thoughts. On this night, perhaps because my mother's voice on the phone has caused a nostalgic wave to pass over me leaving the treasures and debris of the past on my lap, I write about my father.

My father died with many things unspoken between us. Until his death in a car accident during my first year in graduate school, he directed my goals through his own unfulfilled dreams. He was an intellectual who did not go to college, a dreamer without hope, an artist without a medium. So I went to college. I became a teacher and later a writer. I had to finish what he had never even begun at the time of his death. My mother could not bear life in the States without him as her interpreter and companion, so she went home to her Island. She got what she always wanted, but not in the way she wanted. She wanted a return to *la Isla;* she got it, but without him. I stayed behind with my books, my memories.

Knowledge was all the wealth and power my father wanted. His only luxury was our education, my brother's and mine. He invested in us. He bought us books and paid our tuition at private Catholic schools when we could not afford to buy a house. Our times together were precious and rare since his job as a career navy man kept him away from home during my waking hours and sometimes at sea for months. Our talks had to be carved out of the rare Sunday afternoon when he was home on leave—hours for which my mother competed also.

It was a solitary life we led, and I never quite understood why my parents chose to live in a social limbo. In piecing together in my notebooks what my mother talks about more freely now that she has returned to the Island, I began to understand that it was my father who chose to live in this country, and they had not really shared quite the same dream.

As a Puerto Rican family we were voluntary exiles, since we were free to go back to our homeland anytime. We could not even claim economic need because Father had a steady income through the Navy that kept us securely in our lower-middle-class status. The difficult part was that neither of my parents really assimilated into life in the U.S. The place my father chose to settle down was Paterson, New Jersey. Yet we did not stay for long in the rapidly growing Puerto Rican community; instead he rented us an apartment in a Jewish-owned building in a neighborhood of European immigrants where we were an oddity, once more strangers in a strange setting. Though I never experienced racism in its most brutal forms, our exclusion was as evident as a new silence as one enters a room.

I attended a school with the driven and overachieving off-spring of Nazi camp survivors and also alongside the children of Irish and Italian immigrants. It was among them that I learned how to concentrate on one thing at a time until I mastered it. The kids I knew centered their lives not around the normal flirting and cruising of mainstream teenage life, but on their complex family lives and all the attending ceremonies. I felt my loneliness most keenly when a door opened and I heard the up-roar of life shared with others under one roof, a family gathered around a television set, laughing at a joke they all understood, or arguing in one language; when we walked through the door into our own quiet, orderly apartment we had to take off our English at the door as well as our street shoes, for our mother would speak only Spanish and our father was determined that we would not provoke complaints from our neighbors.

My father was a good friend of the owner of our building, an immigrant Jew. The man was of Mediterranean heritage, and his dark features and curly black hair made him look more like a Puerto Rican than my father, who was a thin, fair-skinned man with an elegant bearing. I knew that my father stood out when he walked down our street, where the population was mainly composed of swarthy European men.

My mother hardly ever left our apartment, except twice a month when my father brought his black Oldsmobile out of the downtown garage where he kept it to the front of our building and we went shopping: first to the A&P and then to the Puerto Rican shops in the barrio where my mother bought the ingredients she needed for the dishes she liked to cook. The people in these *bodegas* shot Spanish at one another like machine-gun fire. So fast did they speak that I could barely understand what they were saying. And they stared at the three of us—overdressed by their standards, my mother in her brocaded black coat with the fur collar, my father in a coat and tie or dress Navy blues, and me usually in the pleated skirts and plain white blouses my father liked to see me wear, in my neat cloth coat from Sears. My little brother's outfit was the masculine match for mine: dark trousers, button-up shirt. We were a family who dressed like the models in the store catalogues my father brought home to use as picture dictionaries and my mother studied as manuals of American life. Yet we were suspect to the other customers. Little pockets of silence would form around us as my mother examined the yuccas, plantains, green bananas, and other *viandas* she would need for the week's meals.

I would watch the sharp bones of my father's cheeks and see his jaw clamp down hard. A look of haughty indifference would settle over his face as he "escorted" my mother up and down the aisles crammed with dusty bottles and cans bearing labels in Spanish. He kept his hands in his pockets and followed just behind her left elbow as if to protect her from dangers hidden in the stacks. She walked slowly, picking up cans and reading the labels, perhaps savoring the familiar smells of her culture, the sounds of sloppy Spanish as customers and clerks engaged in the verbal tag called *el gufeo* in barrio slang. It is a game of double entendres, puns, semi-serious insults, and responses that are *típicos*—the usual exchanges for Puerto Ricans in familiar settings. My father ignored the loud voices, the vulgar innuendoes, and the uncontrolled laughter they incited. My mother obviously enjoyed it. Her offbeat humor and her need for laughter are to this day qualities I love about her. In the early days, she was timid in front of my father and the strangers in the barrio. Back on the Island, she is again quick with the word, the quirky metaphor—was she really the poet in the family? I tagged along in the *bodega,* as I did in the American stores, not really grasping until much later why we did not belong to either world: the quiet, clean world of my father, or the intense, confusing locales where my mother seemed most at ease.

In our apartment, especially during the hours that my father was not there, my mother followed certain rituals that got her through each day. At least twice a week, she walked the five blocks to the nearest Catholic Church to attend mass. I accompanied her only on Sundays. We went to the Spanish-language mass celebrated by a priest from China who had been trained to serve as a missionary in Latin America and had somehow ended up in Paterson. He said mass in Latin and delivered passionate sermons in Chinese-accented Castilian Spanish that was just barely comprehensible to the Puerto Ricans, whose dialect resembled his pure speech about as closely as American English does the dialect of the Scottish Highlands. It took faith and concentration to receive the word of God in Spanish from our determined pastor, but my mother relished each lisped word. Her Catholic training in Puerto Rico had been transferred intact to Paterson, where her isolation made her develop the habits of the religious. She yearned for the others who believed what she believed coming together to celebrate custom. It was the comfort of the familiar that she sought in church ceremony and pious rituals. On the days when she did not attend mass, my mother lit candles in front of a popular depiction of the Virgin—the one where she is crushing the snake with a dainty bare foot.

My mother's religious practices included special prayers said on saints' days, candles every Saturday night, all night, left burning in the bathtub (a fire-safety precaution), and rosaries in memory of dead relatives she kept track of through letters and dates marked in calendars; and, of course, she supervised my religious education since the American nuns did not keep the busy liturgical calendar she followed. Every night while I was a small child my mother came into my room to say the prayer to my Guardian Angel with me. I still remember the words: *Angel de mi guarda / dulce compañía / no me desampares de noche ni de día.* Then she would kiss me, and I'd inhale the smell of Maja soap on the skin of her throat. It was a special soap that came in a box of three cakes, each wrapped in a fancy paper depicting a beautiful dark-haired woman in full Spanish costume of red and black satin and lace, an ornate comb and veil on her head, a black fan coyly held against her cheek. I saved the boxes and paper and kept them in my underclothes drawer to give my garments the sensuous aroma my mother imported for herself. Incense and Spanish Castile soap, essence of my mother, scents of my childhood.

But though Catholic ritual filled the gaps in her life as an exile, they did not turn my mother into a dull, predictable person. She was rather an incurable romantic who was addicted to love stories. She read one Corín Tellado (the Spanish-language Danielle Steele of her time) romance novel a week. I was in charge of buying them, at a quarter each, from the only bookstore in Paterson that carried them, Schwartz's Soda Fountain and Drugstore. As the trustee and executor of her literary needs, I had to learn early to memorize covers and titles so that I would not buy one she had already read. After she was through with a book, she'd let me have it, and that is how I learned to read Spanish. The words that I still retain after all these years are mostly flowery adjectives and passionate verbs used to describe the appearance of the heroes (the girl always dark and lovely, the men always elegant and soft-spoken, unless they were the villains—then they were drawn more varied and interestingly). The actions of the protagonist were always performed within the same formula story, told in countless ways. My mother liked to discuss these *cuentos de amor* with me, and we sometimes dramatized the characters, reading aloud to each other as if we were acting in a soap opera. My father objected to my reading this *basura,* "trash." I once heard him threaten to forbid the books in the house.

"She is impressionable, *Querida,*" he spoke in his perfectly enunciated Spanish. He avoided using slang in both languages and sounded like a foreigner when he spoke either. It was the peculiar slowness of his speech and his insistence on the clarity of each word that made him seem cautious in the way he spoke. "As it is, she is not spending enough time studying. Do not distract her with your silly *novelas.*"

"My *silly novelas* are the only reason I do not go crazy in this place, *Querido.* Shall I give them up, too? Should I read only the Bible and the prayer book until I become *loca?*" My mother's voice intensified like those of actresses in the Mexican movies she loved. Behind closed eyes, I visualized her rising from the table, standing before him, trembling in rage in perfect contrast to his infuriatingly calm demeanor.

"*Contrólate, por favor,*" Father usually warned softly. Our apartment was small. He knew that I could be listening, and only when they were arguing did I get a glimpse into the real conditions of our imposed solitude. When I asked directly why they had chosen to leave the Island, or why they had not returned, the answers were always predictable and vague. "We have a better life here." My father would state this with finality. "There is nothing there for us to go back for." I knew that his father was dead, and his mother was a perpetual wanderer with no permanent home, living with one of her sons or the other. But my mother received mail from her many relatives on the Island.

"No, *Hombre*. You will not deprive me of my books. They are not harmful to our daughter, and they are my only company." Her words were meant to imply that she did not need to be so desperately lonely.

"You obviously do not remember your promise to me. Try to forget your idealized Island. It exists only in your dreams. I know that you feel lonely here, but there is no place for us back there. When I asked you to come to Paterson with me you said you would not look back. Do you remember?"

"I was eighteen years old. What did I know about *la maldita soledad* then? *Mi amor,* can it really be that bad for us in our own country?"

"Our life is here. Our family has a future here. There our

daughter would just be another girl waiting to get married. She would just end up a slave to some ignorant man. And our son would have to join the Army or Navy like I did to make a decent living. Then you would never see him either. Do you want that for them?"

"You are wrong to think that the future is hopeless in our own homeland. Just because your father was a tyrant and your mother a martyr . . ."

"Please be careful that you do not go so far that I cannot forgive your words. We had agreed not to mention my unfortunate family past in this house."

"That is another promise you forced from me when I was too young to understand. Other people have tragedies and troubles in their families, and yet they lead normal lives."

"If you are referring to the population of the barrio—they do not lead 'normal' lives. So many of them are like cattle in a pen doing things in a group because they are afraid of venturing out. We are pioneers. We live our own lives and give our children the best opportunity for an education. So we do not socialize very much. I do not need it. You as my wife should not either."

And so it would go around and around. Little hints for me to ponder: names of people I had never met and of places I had never visited would drop into their intense but subdued late-night arguments, which had become a passionate ritual summoning the painful past and casting a spell over our daily struggle—*la lucha*—and my dangerous, unfathomable future. I would gather their whispered words: discarded flowers to keep between the pages of my notebooks, clues to a mystery I hoped someday to solve. I write about tyrants and martyrs, and about lonely women who find solace in books. All the words I heard my parents trade like currency for each other's loyalties, like treaties to be negotiated so that their children might have choices, they are still with me. The memories emerge in my poems and stories like time travelers popping up with a message for me.

But I must first open the door with a ritual.

* * *

I finish grading my students' essays. What they don't know yet about life and literature can fill volumes. I can do something to remedy the gaps. If they are hungry at all for knowledge, I will add a drop to their half-empty or half-full buckets. But how can I fill mine? As I look deeper into myself, I discover that I left the place where my family's well is located. As a writer I am always in the new territory of Myself Alone. I am looking for new lands to discover every time I begin a sentence. I carry nothing but a dowser's wand and my need to make order, to find a few answers. So by recalling kitchen-table conversations in my notebook, re-inventing them as I go along, perhaps I am moving at a snail's pace toward understanding through my poems, stories, and essays.

Time to rest. I go to my bedroom and open the dresser drawer where I keep my notebook. I add several sentences. In the same drawer I also keep votive candles in different colors. I choose a green one. I can hear my mother saying, *verde-esperanza,* meaning that green meant hope; she always said it when she chose a green candle. My candle, bought at the drugstore, smells like a tropical rain forest, or so the label promises. I place it in front of the photograph I took of the statue of La Virgen de Monserrate, patroness of our pueblo. For a long while I watch the shadows dancing in solemn silence on the white wall. I am held by the complex flux of flame, shadow, and reflection blending in a choreographed repetition of motion in precise intervals. I keep my eyes fixed on the flickering show until I fall into a deep sleep I hope will be undisturbed by the dreams and nightmares that I keep locked away in my notebook for future reference. Sometimes, *most* times, I allow a prayer or a poem to drift like sweetly scented candle smoke into me.

The Gift of a *Cuento*

This is the story of a *cuento* that was given to me once upon a time, and then again. *Una vez y dos son tres.* I was thirteen. It was the year when I began to feel like a Cinderella whose needs were being totally ignored by everyone, including the fairy *madrinas* I fantasized would bring me a new, exciting life with the touch of a magic wand. I had read all of the virtue-rewarded-by-marriage-to-a-handsome-prince tales at the Paterson Public Library and was ready for something miraculous to happen to me: beautiful clothes, an invitation to a great party, love. Unfortunately there was a dearth of princes in my life, and I was not exactly the most popular girl at a school socially dominated by Italian and Irish American princesses. Also, that year I was in the throes of the most severe insecurity crisis of my life: besides being extremely thin—"skinny-bones" was my nickname in the barrio—I was the new girl at the Catholic high school where I had been enrolled that fall, one of two Puerto Rican girls in a small, mostly homogenous social world, and I had also recently been prescribed glasses, thick lenses supported by sturdy black frames. After wearing them for only a few weeks, I developed a semipermanent ridge on my nose. I tried to make up for my physical deficiencies by being well read and witty. This worked fine within my talkative *familia* but not at school, among my peers, who did not value eloquence in girls—not more than a well-developed body and prominent social status, anyway.

That Christmas season, the *cuentista* of our family entered my life. My mother's younger brother, who lived in New York, was the black sheep of the family, with a trail of family *cuentos* about his travels, misadventures, and womanizing behind him—which made him immensely attractive to me. His arrival filled our house with new talk, old stories, and music. Tío liked to tell *cuentos,* and he also liked playing his LPs. My mother and he danced to merengues fresh from the Island—which he seemed to be able to acquire before anyone else, and which he carried with him as if they were precious crystal wrapped in layers of newspaper. He was the spirit of Navidad in our house, with just a hint of the Dionysian about him. Tío enjoyed his

Puerto Rican rum, too, so his visits were as short as the festivities because his bachelor habits eventually wore down my mother's patience.

Tío must have sensed my loneliness that year, for he took it upon himself to spend a lot of time with me the week before Christmas. We went for walks around the gray city, now decked out in lights and ornaments like an overdressed woman, and for pizza downtown. He asked me about my social life and I confessed that my *príncipe* had not appeared on our block yet, so I had none.

"Why do you need a prince to have fun?" my uncle asked, laughing at my choice of words. Unlike other adults, he seemed to really listen. Later I understood this was how he learned to tell a story. He told me that I had inherited his and my *abuela*'s gift of the *cuento*. And because he was so unlike my other *cariñoso* relatives, who poured the sweet words on us kids without discrimination or restraint (or honesty, I thought), I believed him. I knew how to tell a good story. My mother had warned me that it was Tío's charm, his ability to flatter and to persuade, that usually got him into trouble. I wanted that power for myself, too. The seductiveness and the power of words enticed me.

His appeal had little to do with physical beauty: he was short, wiry, with a Taíno Indian face. But he was generous to a fault, completely giving of himself. Our family dreaded his recklessness, but we also adored him for the many sacrifices he had made for our sake, the good deeds that I heard about, along with the spicy *cuentos* and the gossip about his complex love life.

"I guess I was thinking of Cinderella." I didn't want Tío to think me a child, but I also wanted him to understand me in a way no one else could. I wanted magic in my life. Poised between a sheltered childhood and the yearnings of approaching adolescence, my dreams were hopelessly entangled with fairy-tale fantasies. The prince was the prize I had learned to want from the things I heard and saw around me.

"La Cinderella. That girl has really made trouble for us men," Tío laughed.

We were standing in front of the drugstore where my mother bought her twenty-five-cent Corín Tellado romances—which I also avidly read. My uncle took my hand and guided me inside the store. The rack of Spanish-language *novelas* was a Christmas tree of romance. Passionate couples kissing on every cover.

"See what women read?" My uncle gave the rack a turn,

making it go round and round, creating the illusion of a moving picture of embraces and phrases like *"la pasión," "corazón y alma," "besos,"* and the constant refrain of *"el amor, el amor, el amor."*

"Mami reads these," I confessed, "and sometimes I do, too."

"They are all Cinderella stories. Every one of them." Tío gave the rack another turn. "The plot is always the same: Poor or unfortunate girl meets rich, unattainable man. After many hardships he discovers that the shoe will fit only the girl whose beauty he had not ever really seen because of her rags. If he is an alcoholic, he stops drinking; if he's a miser, he turns generous; if he's short and fat . . ."

"Don't tell me—he gets skinny and tall!"

"Or at least he learns to act as if he were perfect in every other way."

"So what's wrong with that?"

"La vida no es así." My uncle looked uncharacteristically solemn when he told me that the expectations of Cinderella and her female followers were simply not the way life really was for men and women, not even when they were in love.

But I didn't hear him. I knew only that my charming *tío*

smelled enticingly of liquor and cigarettes when he leaned down to kiss me, and that he had other vices I could not yet name. But all of that made him alluring to me—the good Catholic girl waiting for life to begin happening for her. He was the mysterious man in one of my mother's *novelas.* I thought he was so much more interesting than my dull, hardworking father and my other male relatives. I didn't know of my *tío's* lifelong battle with alcoholism, or of the throat cancer that would silence his seductive voice forever before he was much older than I am now.

I remember walking with him past the decorated storefronts of downtown Paterson one evening. My uncle made a game of asking me if I wanted this or that for Christmas: a Thumbelina doll like I had desperately wished for last year? No. I had received a hard plastic doll from one of my grandmothers in Puerto Rico, and my parents had decided that that was enough dolls for me. Only Tío had understood that the Thumbelina baby doll *felt* like a real flesh-and-blood baby. We had gone into the store and held it. He had not bought it for me because that year was one of his *años pobres,* when he was between jobs, holing up or drying out at a relative's apartment somewhere, waiting until he could get together enough money to return to *la Isla*. But this year he had money for gifts, he said. Did I want jewelry? We looked at all the shiny baubles in the jewelry store window. No. An *azabache* to wear around my neck to ward off the evil eye? No. I laughed. I was too sophisticated then for such superstitious nonsense.

"Surprise me, Tío."

That week before Nochebuena I stayed close to his magical presence, taking in his masculine appeal, watching women's faces soften when he cast his dark eyes on them, smelling his dangerous other life when he kissed me on the cheek as he said good night and went off like the sleek cat he was to prowl the streets and return in the morning to my mother's kitchen, where his face revealed that he had been *doing* exciting things while the rest of us only dreamed about them.

Mami would frown through her first cup of coffee, then break down in girlish giggles when Tío told us a new joke or *cuento* he had picked up in his wanderings. I gathered these stories in my memory and brought them out during the loneliest times of my life. They nourished and comforted me as they had my mother, who was always hungry for words in Spanish during those first years away from the Island. I had no idea then that my uncle was using his storytelling in a similar way: to trade for attention, time, even affection from others.

"*Mira,* it was like this," he would say, sitting across from my mother at her little Formica table, both of them smoking cigarettes and drinking coffee. "The girl needed attention and I gave her some. I will tell you from the beginning so that you know I am not the scoundrel you think. This is *la verdad, la pura verdad.*"

This phrase was a key to their family joke. Whenever any of my *abuela*'s children started a story with the announcement that it was the pure, unadulterated truth, as the old lady always did before one of her *cuentos,* we all knew that it was going to be a good one. A whopper. No holds barred.

"And how was I to know that she was married? All I knew was that her big brown eyes, like my *sobrina*'s there, were beckoning to me from across the dance floor. *Socorro. Ayuda,* they said to me, save me from this lonely life. . . ."

"She had very eloquent eyes." My mother might comment in mock seriousness.

"What could I do but respond to her silent cries for help?"

"If someone's eyes cry out for help, *pues,* you must do what you have to do, *hombre.*" My mother fell easily into the straight-man role that played such a large part in these entertainments. Their jokes and *cuento*-tellings were more like little plays extemporized by people who knew each other well.

"I did what any man with a heart would have done. I danced a few numbers with her. I bought her a drink. I asked her if she would like me to escort her home. You know the streets of this city . . ."

"Are crawling with criminals!" my mother offered.

"Exactly. Well, that's when she thanked me by telling me that her fiancé was getting off from a late shift at any moment. And . . . well, wasn't that him at the door now? Yes, it was the fiancé at the door, and he looked more like King Kong than any other man I have ever seen. *Hija,* he was covered with black fur from head to toe, and he was so huge that he had to squeeze in through the double doors. Good thing that slowed him down enough so I could end my dance with the lovely *señorita* as quickly as possible."

"But how did you get the egg on your forehead, *hermano?* Did you bump it on your way out?"

"*¡Ay, bendito!* King Kong gave me this little gift. You see there was no back door. And for a big ape, the fiancé moved fast. The only thing I regret is that he wasted a perfectly good bottle of

Bacardi by using it as a weapon on my head."

"Maybe it was not all wasted," my mother was giggling and I was, too, by then. "I think it may have seeped into your brain through your pores."

While I listened to my mother and my uncle talk, I saw how all their daily struggles ceased for the time it took to tell the *cuento,* how pleased they were with their own wit, their ability to laugh at disappointments and hurts and, best of all, to transform any ordinary episode into an adventure.

On Christmas Eve the family gathered in our living room. My mother and I had polished the green linoleum floor until it was a mirror reflecting the multicolored lights of the Christmas tree, which had done its job of perfuming our apartment with the aroma of evergreen. I was wearing a red party dress my mother had let me choose from her closet and a pair of her pumps. I looked at least eighteen, I thought. I put some of Tío's *pachanga* records on our turntable and waited anxiously for him to come through the door with my gift. What I expected it to be was in the airy realm of a dream. But it would, I knew without a doubt, be magical.

It was late when he finally showed up bearing a brown grocery bag full of gifts and a bleached-blond woman on his arm. After kissing his sisters, waving to me from across the room, and wishing everyone *Felices Pascuas,* he and his partner left for another party. My mother and aunts shook their heads at their brother's latest caprice. My feet hurt in the high-heeled shoes, so I sat out the dances and read one of my mother's books. Sometime around midnight I was handed my gifts. Among them there was an unwrapped box of perfume with a card from my uncle. The perfume was Tabu. The card read: "*La Cenisosa* from our Island does not get a prince as a reward. She has another gift given to her. I heard a woman tell this *cuento* once. Maybe you can find it in the library or ask Mamá to tell it to you when you visit her next time."

My mother thought the perfume was too strong for a girl my age and would not let me wear it. I was disappointed by the gift, but I would occasionally spray on the perfume anyway. I discovered that its wilted-flower scent triggered my imagination. I could imagine myself in many different ways when I smelled it. It was the kind of perfume no one else would give me.

I did not find the *cuento* of *La Cenisosa* in the Paterson Public Library, nor in any other book collection for many years. Recently I ran across an anthology of *cuentos folklóricos* from

Puerto Rico, and there it was: *La Cenisosa*. In *La Cenisosa* of Puerto Rico, Cinderella is rewarded by a family of three *hadas madrinas,* fairy godmothers, for her generosity of spirit, but her prize is not the hand of a prince. Instead, she is rewarded with diamonds and pearls that fall from her mouth whenever she opens it to speak. And she finds that she can be brave enough to stand up to her wicked stepmother and stepsisters and clever enough to banish them from her home forever. Around the time when I translated this folktale my mother wrote to say that my uncle was dying from cancer of the throat back on the Island where they had both returned years before. She said that his voice was almost totally gone but not his indomitable spirit. He knew he had little time left to give us the words he wanted us to remember. He had my mother write to me and tell me that he had read my novel and wanted me to know that my stories gave him pleasure. He sent me his *bendición.* I took his blessing to mean that he had accepted my gift of words.

Woman in Front of the Sun

As the plane taxis to the gate in San Juan, the sun pours in through the windows in waves and I have to reach blindly into my bag for my dark glasses. There are shouts of *"Mira, Mira!"* and excited conversations. Immediately I can feel the strangely physical way I am changed when I arrive on this island. It is a flutter in my chest, an excitement, a feeling of joyful anticipation. It's almost like falling in love, or maybe the start of a fever.

I step out of the cabin into light so intense that the attendant at the bottom of the steps is transformed into an outline of a woman against the white field of the runway: a shadow figure—as in Miró's painting *Woman in Front of the Sun*. Almost instantly my skin dampens with perspiration; my body is desperately trying to adjust to the heat and humidity. Perhaps the feeling of excitement is merely biological: my autonomic nervous system taking over and alerting my heart of the extra load it will have to carry. I know just enough science to make me an uncomfortable traveler. It reminds me of the time when I was a know-it-all college freshman. I would try to explain the concept of evolution to my mother over the telephone, try to convince her that empirical truth was better than religion. I told her that love and sex were only nature's way of preserving the species. She let me show off my erudition for as long as she could stand it, then dismissed the absurd idea that love was regulated by our brain chemicals. She thought that Darwin, Freud, and anyone else who was foolish enough to try to diminish the miracles of love and childbirth was obviously a fool. *El destino* is responsible for all that happens in our lives, both good and bad. *El Destino y la Providencia*—Destiny and Providence—are my mother's twin muses.

The dizzying heat of a Puerto Rican summer is another subject she refuses to discuss. It is a part of her *destino*. Talking about it, *thinking* about it, *is* what makes one perspire profusely, she claims. I suspect she does know something about physiological responses; but like a yogi, she simply turns her systems on and off at will. Here is the empirical evidence.

Her makeup never runs as mine does. She lives without air-conditioning and does not languish as I do. And I now know that I will not ever succeed in educating her out of the blind faith that keeps her cool while I pant and lose the precious liquids that support life.

Although the San Juan airport has been modernized over the years I have been visiting Puerto Rico, it still retains its island character. The music playing over the sound system is definitely not Muzak. I find myself humming along with a rumba instrumental I recognize from my childhood.

Checking the monitor, I see that the next shuttle flight to Mayagüez, the airport closest to my *pueblo,* is two hours away. I head for the *fritura* stand on the bottom level where I can sit in the open courtyard, have a strong *café con leche,* and watch people come and go. I have written many poems and letters here while waiting for flights to my mother's house. I take in like drugs the ocean breeze blowing in from the bay and the knock-you-down wafts of the aroma of fritters simmering in olive oil on the grill. Then there is the pervasive music, salsa over the PA, over countless radios perched over every work area.

People do not adjust the volume; they conduct their business above it.

I read somewhere that love of *la patria* is an intrinsic part of the Puerto Rican psyche, very much connected to self-identity, and that this is why it was impossible to fully Americanize the Island during the years—my parents' school years—when the American governors attempted to force a shift to English as the main language through the classrooms. There was passive resistance to the whole concept.

I see a sort of rebellion now: even as the young people claim their right to the pervasive rock-and-roll culture, the music that rules the air waves is still mainly homegrown. It is a matter of pride for people of all ages here to master the intricate steps and sensuous movements of the Island dances. It is still amazing for me to see a couple in their seventies at a public dance hall holding each other tightly while swaying to a sexy mambo. When I was a child, the celebrations in our family—the birthdays, baptisms, anniversaries—were some of my favorite times. At some point in the evening my mother would leave the other women who congregated in the kitchen and persuade my father to dance with her. In his elegant way he would waltz her around the room. Cheek-to-cheek, like new lovers, they would dance together as if they had no troubles. And perhaps for the length of the sensuous *bolero,* they didn't. I listen as the woman emptying trash cans sings passionately along with the radio she takes around in her pushcart. There are spontaneous bursts of song from the airport personnel that anywhere else would call for odd looks and perhaps alarmed reactions by employers. Music is the opiate of this people. Everyone is "on" it, and it's free.

The airport in San Juan makes me feel as if I were in a market-place in Morocco. The place is a veritable crossroads for the Caribbean, and the faces cover a wide spectrum, from the lobster-pink Dutch businessman on his way to the Virgin Islands to the quietly excited Japanese couple on holiday. But the two who interest me sit at the little table to my right. They are obviously college students with the obligatory backpacks parked by their chairs. The girl is Puerto Rican; I can tell by her slight Spanish accent, similar to mine, which has been almost neutralized by American city intonations. The boy appears to be the old-money-preppie type: perfect teeth and a clear complexion, expensive rearing. He is tanned, athletic, and obviously besotted by his companion. But by Island standards he is inappropriately dressed for a first meeting in his shorts and T-shirt. Especially for a foreigner. Clothes speak volumes here. She is nervous. Her hand is on his shoulder in a possessive gesture; she is drilling him on what to say and not to say when they arrive at her family's home.

The man at the counter waves to me; my order is ready: cod fritters, rice, and red beans. My health- and fitness-conscious daughter would lecture me sternly if she could see what I am about to consume. She would point out that grease is the fatal flaw in Puerto Rican cuisine. She would describe in graphic detail how my arteries are going to clog up like old sewer lines. Though I know the sermon verbatim, I dig in. My adipose cells yell, ¡Olé! My body celebrates the orgy of oil and fat and spices. The taste and aroma of the meal take me back to my primal Puerto Rican self.

The young lovers at the *fritura* stand finish their meal. She begs him, please—when they get to her home—to allow her father to do most of the talking, to eat anything that is put in front of him by her mother, and to just ignore her younger sister, who will try to flirt with him. Of course, they will have separate rooms. He grins mischievously at her when she mentions the sleeping arrangements. She nervously glances around to see if anyone has seen or heard their exchange. I keep my head down over my plate, but I watch them out of the corners of my eyes. He nods at everything she says, and sighs deeply as they rise from the table. "Time to head for the gate, Maggie," he says, grabbing both of their backpacks and slinging them over his muscular shoulders.

"Don't forget to call me Margarita when we get to my house. My father hates my American name," she warns him. I see him shake his head in dismay. She slips her arm through his, and standing on her toes kisses him on the lips. "You'll be fine, *mi amor,*" she says.

Glancing at my watch, I see that it's time for me to head for my gate, too. I have always enjoyed the short flight across the Island in the low-flying little propeller planes. The gorgeous contrast of emerald landscapes and turquoise sea, it seems to be within my hand's grasp, as though I could reach out of the little window and grab it all like a handful of gems to take with me and bring out like a child's marbles on a gray day.

I make my way through the crowded airport, hearing people call out to each other from one end to another as if they were in a park: greetings, arguments, deals, and declarations all tossed unguarded and unchecked back and forth. Halfway to my gate I pass an automatic door, which opens, and the wave of humid, oven-hot air calls me outside. Stepping into the sun, I am momentarily blinded by a white light that makes everything seem like a mirage. The palm trees lining the road are in such fluid motion that for a moment I feel that I am on the deck of a ship. This effect of group consciousness, of movement choreographed to a frenetic underscore, is all part of my earliest memories of the Island; it has always seemed to me that this place is somehow more alive than the roomy mainland, buzzing like a beehive, teeming with lives being lived in close proximity. I am drawn to it, caught in it. The intense hum of my beginnings has made its usual unexpected connection with my brain or my heart; I will soon not remember the difference. There is no way I cannot follow the song that reaches me at the cellular level, changing me chemically as it becomes a part of my blood, my nervous system. I believe I have arrived home, and my whole being knows it.

I visit my mother in Puerto Rico every year. One year I arrived at her home the day before a monster hurricane *organized* itself to strike the Lesser Antilles. Napoleon was at the gates and I had arrived for the reception. My mother greeted me as warmly as ever and then suggested that I help her put things away in boxes and plastic bags. I turned on her TV to CNN—*SEH, EHNNE, y EHNNE* is the new Big Brother, constantly informing us, whether we want to hear it or not, of doom, in progress or impending. I showed Mami the satellite photos of Hurricane Luis, the aptly named macho storm that was going to gobble up our little island as a snack before it moved on to hardier fare.

"No use packing," I said to her in my most ominous Spanish, "we are all going to die."

"Turn off the *televisor, hija,*" she advised me gently but firmly. "It is God who determines when our time has come, not *SEH, EHNNE, y EHNNE.*"

"They are *predicting* our fate, Mami, not determining it." I had easily fallen for the trap she always lays for me. This woman with ten fewer years of formal education is as wily in her semantic entrapments as any sophistical intellectual I have met. Her point is always the same: to prove that if I only had faith, *La Fe* (which is to say, the one *she* practices), I would surely lead a better life.

"They are predicting the future, are they? Is it like when I go see a spiritist and she tells me when I will take a long trip, who is my enemy, how to interpret my dreams, and what numbers I should play *en la lotería nacional?* I remember the last lecture you gave me, soon after I won that group lottery at the Optimistas Club, with my special number. You talked about it all being *coincidencia.*"

"That's different. This weather prediction is based on scientific data."

"Well, I'm not ready to die. We will have plenty of time to talk later. Help me pack these things and prepare some bottled water."

"Supplies, Mami?" I decided to give her a bit of the same *medicina.* "Why should we bottle water if God does not intend to smite us but only to scare the hell out of us by letting the beast breathe in our faces?"

"Hija, Dios aprieta pero no ahoga." Her tone was as patiently condescending as she could manage. Our parts in these discussions are by now polished and professional.

God will tighten his grip, but he will not strangle.

We could have gone on, and have, for hours on God's vagueness. Why does God tighten his grip on our throats? I would certainly ask her. Why won't he strangle? And she would have an answer or an appropriate proverb for everything.

So we packed while God tightened his grip. The things she chose to put away in her "heavy duty" plastic bags were mostly predictable. She has no jewels or invaluable *objets d'art*. She packed the bulging family albums with pictures that she could use to connect the dots of our family life: this was taken before or after your Papi's death, during the Cuban Missile Crisis, after we moved to *los Estados Unidos,* before your father became ill, when you were two, five, a *quinceañera* . . . . And so on. The other items were her talismans and totems. The religious objects that she had carried with her from apartment to apartment on the mainland, little house to little house on the Island as a Navy wife and later as a widow upon her final return to her homeland. I got caught up in the ritual. I handed her what she asked for like an acolyte in a ceremony, my mother a priestess going from station to station of our lives, making each ordinary event meaningful by telling its story.

In the poem I wrote about this incident I tell of the feeling of grace that I attained in the presence of sacred activity that I recognized in my mother's preparations before the storm. She was doing what I attempt to do when I work on a poem, story, or essay. I attempt to make the ordinary rise toward all its symbolic potential. I try to make art out of the only material I have available to me, my life and what I have learned from living it and examining it. My mother was trying to save the markers to the anthology of her life. After writing "Before the Storm," I understood this and began to see her in a different way. In her company that day while we waited for the beast to do its (or God's) will, I saw her as my fellow artist. I finally understood that I have always loved and admired this woman who is so culturally different from me, whose language gives me pause, whose joy of life I can never match, and who delights in proving me wrong in my elevated notions of life and the world, because she is my fellow artist. And this led to the larger revelation that the state of grace I felt, which I had always attributed to the creative act, is available to all who have come to meaning in their lives. So my tune changed on that day before the storm. I no longer felt privileged because I had found access to the fulfillment that only writing gives me. She and I had both found a way to give meaning to our lives, and it was the same for both of us. We collected the materials for our collage, we looked for possible patterns emerging from the pieces, we organized them in a way that seemed right to us, and finally we hoped that the others, whose view of our work mattered to us, saw its beauty and value.

As the last bag was filled my mother said, "Did I ever tell you the story of how your grandmother was lifted off the ground by the winds of *el huracán San Felipe?* She was skinny like you and crossing the pasture when she was caught by the wind, and she flew high enough to see the whole pueblo below."

I had heard the story before, but I obediently sat in my mother's rocker facing the muted television showing the approach of the killer storm and listened for the revised, new version. In the last telling it had been my *abuela*'s long skirts that had become a parachute, allowing her to levitate just long enough to cause her to have a recurrent dream of flight for the rest of her life. Today she was destined to be granted more air time by my mother.

Woman in Front of the Sun

Before the Storm

HURRICANE LUIS, PUERTO RICO, 1995

We are talking in whispers
about what is worth saving. A box of photographs
is pushed under the bed, and the rendering
of Jesus knocking at somebody's door, a hesitant young man,
that arrived with us in each new house, and another
of his dear mother holding his poor broken body
not many years later, are taken down
from their precarious places on the walls.
We surprise each other with our choices.
She fills boxes
while I watch the sky for signs, though I feel,
rather than see, nature is readying
for the scourge. Falling silent, the birds seek safety
in numbers, and the vagabond dogs cease their begging
for scraps. The avocados are dropping
from the laden trees in her backyard
as if by choice. Bad weather always brings in a good crop
of the water-fruit, she tells me; it is the land
offering us a last meal.

Woman in Front of the Sun

On the outer islands, the fragile homes of the poor
are already in its jaws, the shelters we see on film,
all those bodies huddled in the unnatural dark, the wind howling
like a hungry dog in the background, make us stand solemn.
In the mainland my family and friends will watch
the satellite pictures of this storm with trepidation
as it unravels over the Caribbean. But I am already too close
to see the whole picture. Here, there is
a saturated mantle descending,
a liquid fullness in the air, like a woman feels
before the onset of labor. Finally,
the growing urgency of the sky, and I am strangely excited,
knowing that I am as ready as I will ever be,
should I have another fifty years to go,
to go with my mother
toward higher ground. And when we come home, if
we come home, if there's a home where we believe
we left one, it will all be different.

Taking the Macho

There is a legend not recorded in history books that in 1496 when Columbus's ships landed on a tiny Caribbean island so that his crew could refresh themselves, the men were confronted by a tribe of fierce women. Dressed for battle, wearing the plumage of warriors, they "assumed a menacing attitude" in front of the longboats. Astonished—and perhaps also amused by the sight—the men begged the women to allow them to come ashore to rest and eat.

Fernando Colón, the admiral's son, tells in his biography of his father that the women ordered the sailors to go away, telling them that if they wanted supplies they could sail on to the north shore of the island where there were men who would help them.

But the sea-weary mariners were through playing games by this time. The women's refusal of hospitality was an insult to their macho. So they opened fire on them with their guns. Then they looted the women's village, destroyed what they found, and took the remaining women warriors captive. The women put up such a fight that the admiral was moved to note their "strange fury." According to Fernando Colón a woman *cacique,* one of the chiefs of the tribe, almost killed "a courageous Canary islander": "She tried to make him prisoner; she grappled with him, threw him to the ground and would have choked him if the other Christians had not come to his aid."

The Christians were not so much impressed as affronted by the fierceness of these *unnatural* females. The captive women told the admiral, his son reports, that these women had husbands but did not live with them. *They* would summon the men when they wanted to "lie with them." And these were brief, purposeful encounters that were determined by the women. Fernando Colón had very likely read of the mythological Amazons of classical legends, so he did not doubt the existence of these macho women of the Conquistadors' tales. He also believed in sea monsters and lost cities of gold.

It is not surprising that his writings have been selectively discounted by historians. No sea serpent, no macho women.

We do have exhaustive studies of the lives of ordinary women in Spanish colonial times: the pious, submissive white women and the aboriginal women beaten by history into silence and obscurity and into passive acceptance of the inevitable. The courage, even macho, of the aboriginal women were no match for disease, enslavement, rape, and genocide. A few surviving native women married white men and became the mothers of a new race that lived according to the rules of their conquerors once Christianity was established on the Island. It took only a couple of generations before the Indian population of my native island of Puerto Rico was decimated to a few hundred native people who managed to escape into the mountains. It was not long before no pure-blood native was to be found anywhere on the Island. The women of the Conquistadors were not bred for macho; they were ladies. And the only females who could have laid claim to the term had vanished into legend—or to the mountains to die.

In the dictionary, the noun "macho" is defined as the male of the species. However, it is the modifier that interests me, as in "macho man"; literally translated that means "male man"—a redundancy, or an indication that the adjective can also be attached to another noun, such as "macho woman"?

What were the Caribbean women warriors defending? It was their territory, that is obvious. No mention is made of any raids and warfare initiated by these women. They apparently *asked* their men to mate with them, and they donned their warrior plumage only when they saw invaders approaching. Because historians have determined for us that this is a legend, I take the liberty of interpreting it from my perspective as a woman fiercely protective of her artistic and personal territory. I believe that this tribe of women had made a choice to take control of their lives, including their reproductive function, which they managed by deciding for themselves when they wanted to "lie with their husbands." I can imagine how horrified Columbus's Christians must have been at the very idea, and why they had to bring out their big guns against these women. When you see an aberration, you cross yourself, commend your soul to God, and shoot it.

The interesting thing is that matriarchy in the Caribbean is a historical fact, a system that had functioned for the native people until the Discovery. There is some evidence of the existence of a very powerful tribal chief, a woman *cacique* named Loiza whose region was on the banks of what is now called the Rio Grande de Loiza. This river was sacred to the Indians of

Borinquen—the name the Indios gave to the island before the gold-crazy Spaniards renamed it Puerto Rico—because it was where many of the spirits they worshipped lived. Loiza was said to have the power to invoke the spirit that brought good rain and helped the crops to grow. Her male counterpart was the god of storms called Juracan (or Huracan). His fury was devastation. Although her name lives on as that of a great river, the *cacique* Loiza has faded into legend. It is difficult to prove that she existed at all, although anthropologists have found evidence of a strong matriarchal society that linked the indigenous tribes of the Island. Their religion was based on the Earth Mother, with the belief that a balance of the male and female elements was the source of harmony in their world.

Anthropologists have speculated that women also participated in the sacred ball games played in the *bateyes* (ball courts) that have been excavated and reconstructed in this century. Fernández de Oviedo in his *General and Natural History of the Indies,* written in the sixteenth century, claims that the games, which were staged as fertility rites, were "usually played by teams of men, or of women, and sometimes teams of both sexes," and that "on still other occasions women played against men and married women against the unmarried." The object of the games reported by the eyewitness de Oviedo was for both women and men to appeal to the gods with their beauty and power. De Oviedo himself seems to have been impressed by the scene: "It is amazing," he wrote, "to see the speed and agility of both sexes."

It was a wondrous *and* disturbing sight for the macho Conquistadors to see women and men going into battle together and playing *pelota* on the same team! The quintessential male game of baseball is often colloquially referred to as *pelota* on the Island today. Women do not play *pelota* (ball). Why? The most memorable answer I ever got from a man was: "Because women do not have *pelotas* (balls)." And laughter.

Perhaps because the only world that the Spaniards who colonized the island of my birth could conceive of was one dominated by *pelotas*-equipped machos, I was born into a culture that determined a woman's value by how well she fitted her predetermined feminine role. I felt its constraints from the start, but especially after I discovered that my artistic drive often clashed with male macho. You cannot be passive and *create*. Even the famous examples of women who stayed home and were artists do not mean that these women were passive. Emily Dickinson's life was in her own words "a loaded gun."

The ones who are forced into frustrated silence may end up dashing their brains upon the moors, speculated Virginia Woolf, or simply giving up the Gargantuan struggle and settling for being the Angel in the House. Woolf said she continuously tried to kill this solicitous creature so that she could get on with her life as an artist. We can get us to a nunnery, where we might be allowed an ecstatic vision or two on an approved subject. Or we can claim our share of macho and confront the longboats.

Using the word "macho" to modify "woman" may be a call to semantic controversy. Can a woman have "macho"? Does she need it? After all, she can have her choice of many other less-loaded epithets that mean courage, that mean essentially the same as this masculine modifier. But not quite the same. According to the books, it took "macho" to conquer the New World, the "right stuff"—Anglo for "macho"—to explore space and travel to the moon. It takes balls to do anything dangerous and new, or so it seems. But we may be able to transform an anatomical fact into a useful metaphor. And maybe we need to liberate the word, because unless we can claim macho we may be doomed to a degree less of what we need for this dangerous exploration of inner space called artistic creation.

This is "macho": On his transatlantic flight Charles Lindbergh flew a specially designed airplane, the *Spirit of St. Louis,* that allowed him no forward visibility (he did not want to be trapped between cabin and fuselage in an emergency so he had the cockpit built far back in the aircraft). He crossed the ocean with *no forward visibility.* This is the kind of macho that best serves the artist. It involves no call to battle. It is an act of pure courage, an act of daring that straddles the line between heroism and foolish bravado. It is done because it is both necessary and unnecessary. If Lindbergh had not crossed the Atlantic, someone else would have. But he had to do it. It was necessary to *him.*

We all walked into that space shuttle with Christa McAuliffe. But did we become part of the sky with her? It took something greater than courage for both of these people to step into the unknown. Success, or in their case survival, was not guaranteed. There are no guarantees. That is the only guarantee in a life dedicated to discovery. Next to death, failure may be the thing that we fear the most. This morning, every morning, when I sit down to fill a page with my best efforts at making language a viable medium for my being, I walk into the unknown. I do not face death in the way the real-world adventurers Charles Lindbergh and Christa McAuliffe did, but I too fly without a map, and I have known paralyzing fear. Writing exposes me to the world, daring it to accept me in spite of the fact that I have an overwhelming need to expose its many foibles and failings. The writer is the matador of the empty ring. We incite the beast to attack us, displaying as much red—the color of macho—as we dare, then we hope we are agile enough to avoid its horns— *Por Dios*—one more time. By the time the spectators arrive at the arena, we have retreated to tend to our wounds. All they see is the fire-breathing animal we say we created. Sometimes the crowd waves white handkerchiefs and the monster lives. Other times they walk away in disgust, seeing nothing more than a tired old cow where we had left—or so we believed— *verdad*—we really did—the Minotaur.

The writer sits down before a blank page, the painter faces the empty canvas, the sailor sets out toward the edge of the world, the aviator points his craft in the general direction of another continent, a teacher boards a spaceship, anyone steps out of his or her safe home into the traffic. Who is the wisest? Who will sleep sound and safe in their own beds tonight? There are no guarantees.

Yet most of us would like to believe that we lead sane lives and that we will not come to harm or evil if we do not go out and seek it. The artist goes out, or rather, she goes *in* and finds what disturbs her and what possesses her, and she wrestles with it. She transforms herself into that macho woman that Columbus's son was astonished by: "she tried to make *him* prisoner" (my emphasis). Fernando Colón, like his father and his men, was offended at this unnatural reversal of macho rules: a woman warrior was to him an oxymoron, a contradiction in terms. Didn't this *India* know that a woman cannot conquer a Conquistador? That only men can have macho? No, she had not yet been *civilized,* so she believed that if she needed macho, she could summon it out of herself, and that's why she fought back.

The Woman Who
Slept with One Eye Open

As a child caught in that lonely place between two cultures and two languages, I wrapped myself in the magical veil of folktales and fairy tales. The earliest stories I heard were those told by the women of my family in Puerto Rico, some of the tales being versions of Spanish, European, and even ancient Greek and Roman myths that had been translated by time and by each generation's needs into the *cuentos* that I heard. They taught me the power of the word. These *cuentos* have been surfacing in my poems and my prose since I decided to translate them for myself and to use them as my palette, the primary colors from which all creation begins.

The stories that have become the germinal point for not only my work as a creative artist but also my development as a free woman are those of two women. One is María Sabida, "the smartest woman on the whole island," who conquered the heart of a villain and "slept with one eye open." And the other is María Sabida's opposite, María La Loca, the woman who was left at the altar, the tragic woman who went crazy as a result of a broken heart. Once a beautiful girl, María La Loca ends up, in my grandmother's *cuento,* a pitiful woman who retreats into insanity because she is shamed by a man, cheated out of the one option she allowed herself to claim: marriage.

The crude and violent tale of María Sabida, which I have found in collections of folktales recorded from the oral tellings of old people at the turn of the century, revealed to me the amazing concept that a woman can have "macho"—that quality that men in certain countries, including my native island, have claimed as a male prerogative. The term "macho," when divested of gender, to me simply means the arrogance to assume that you belong where you choose to stand, that you are inferior to no one, and that you will defend your domain at whatever cost. In most cases, I do not recommend this mode as the best way to make room for yourself in a crowded world. But I grew up in a place and time where modesty and submissiveness were the qualities a girl was supposed to internalize. So the woman who slept with one eye open intrigued me as a possible model in my formative years as a creative artist. Of course, it would be a long time before I articulated what I knew then instinctively: María Sabida's "macho" was what I myself would need to claim for my art. It is almost bravado to say "I am a writer" in a society where that condition usually means "I am unemployed," "I live on the fringes of civilization," "I am declaring myself better/different," and so forth. I know writers who will put anything else under "occupation" on a passport or job application rather than call up a red flag of distrust that the word "writer" has come to have for many people.

When I feel that I need a dose of "macho," I follow a woman's voice back to María Sabida. I have come to believe that she was the smartest woman on the island because she learned how to use the power of words to conquer her fears; she knew that this was what gave men their aura of power. They knew how to convince themselves and others that they were brave. Of course, she still had to sleep with one eye open because when you steal secrets, you are never again safe in your bed. María Sabida's message may be entirely different to me from what it was to the generations of women who heard and told the old tale. As a writer I choose to make her my alter ego, my *comadre*. In Catholic cultures two women otherwise unrelated can enter into a sacred bond, usually for the sake of a child, called the *comadrazgo*. One woman swears to stand in for the other as a surrogate mother if the need arises. It is a sacrament that joins them, more sacred than friendship, more binding than blood. And if these women violate the trust of their holy alliance, they will have committed a mortal sin. Their souls are endangered. I feel similarly about my commitment to the mythical María Sabida. My *comadre* taught me how to defend my art, how to conquer the villain by my wits. If I should ever weaken my resolve, I will become María La Loca, who failed herself, who allowed herself to be left at the altar.

Comadres y compadres, let me tell you the *cuento* of María Sabida, the smartest woman on the whole island.

Once upon a time, there was a widower merchant who had no other children, only a daughter. He often had to leave her alone while he traveled on business to foreign lands. She was called María Sabida because she was smart and daring and knew how to take care of herself. One day, the merchant told her that he would be away on a trip for a long time and left María Sabida in the company of her women friends.

One moonless night when she and her *compañeras* were sitting on the veranda of her father's house talking, María Sabida saw a bright light in the distance. Because the house was far away from the pueblo, she was very curious about what the light could be. She told her friends that they would investigate the source of light the very next morning.

As planned, early the next day, María Sabida and her friends set out through the woods in the direction where they had seen the light. They arrived at a house that seemed to be unoccupied. They went in and peered into each room. It looked like a man's place. But they smelled cooking. So they followed their noses to the kitchen, where an old man was stirring a huge cauldron. He welcomed them and asked them to stay and eat. María Sabida looked in the pot and saw that it was filled with the arms and legs of little children. Then she knew that this was the house of a gang of killers, kidnappers, and thieves that had been terrorizing the countryside for years. Sickened by the sight, María Sabida picked up the pot and poured its contents out of the window. The old man screamed at her: "You will pay for this, woman! When my master comes home, he will kill you and your *compañeras!*" Then at gunpoint he led them upstairs where he locked them up.

When the leader of the thieves arrived with his gang, María Sabida heard him conspiring with his men to trick the women. Bearing a tray of *higos de sueño,* sleep-inducing figs, the *jefe* came up to the bedroom where the women were being kept. In a charming voice he persuaded the women to eat the fruit. María Sabida watched her friends fall deeply asleep one by one. She helped the *jefe* settle them in beds as she planned. Then she pretended to eat a fig and lay down yawning.

To test how well the potion in the fruit had worked, the *jefe* of the thieves lit a candle and dripped a few drops of hot wax on the women's faces. María Sabida bore the pain without making a sound.

Certain now that the women were deeply asleep, the *jefe* went to the second-floor veranda and whistled for his comrades to come into the house. María Sabida leaped from the bed as he was leaning over the rail, and she pushed him off. While his men were tending to their injured leader, María Sabida awakened the women and they followed her to safety.

When María Sabida's father returned from his journey days later, she told him that she had decided to marry the leader of the thieves. The father sent a letter to the man asking him if he would marry his daughter. The *jefe* responded immediately that he had been unable to forget the smart and brave María Sabida. Yes, he would marry her. The wedding took place with a great fiesta. Everyone in the pueblo hoped that María Sabida would reform this criminal and that they could stop fearing his gang. But as soon as the couple had arrived at the thieves' house, the new husband told his bride that now she would pay for having humiliated him in front of his men. He told her to go to the bedroom and wait for him. María Sabida knew that he was going to murder her. She had an idea. She asked her husband if he would let her take some honey to eat before she went to bed. He agreed. And while he drank his rum and celebrated her death with his gang, María

Sabida worked in the kitchen making a life-size honey doll out of burlap sacks. She filled the doll with honey, cutting off some of her own hair to affix to its head. She even tied a string to its neck so that she could make the doll move from where she planned to hide under the marriage bed. She took the honey doll upstairs and placed it on the bed. Then she slid underneath the bed where she could see the door.

It was not long before the husband came in drunk and ready for blood. He struck the honey doll, thinking that it was María Sabida. He insulted her and asked if she thought she was smart now. Then he plunged a dagger into the doll's heart. A stream of honey hit him on the face. Tasting the sweetness on his mouth and tongue, the assassin exclaimed: "María Sabida, how sweet you are in death, how bitter in life. If I had known your blood contained such sweetness, I would not have killed you!"

María Sabida then came out from under the bed. In awe that María Sabida had outsmarted him again, the leader of the thieves begged her to forgive him. María Sabida embraced her husband. They lived happily together, so they say. But on that night of her wedding, and every other night, María Sabida slept with one eye open.

I have translated the tale of María Sabida several times for different purposes, and each time the story yields new meanings. Time and again the words I use to roughly equate the powerful

Spanish change meanings subtly as if the story were a Ouija board, drawing letters out of my mind to form new patterns. This is not hocus-pocus. It is the untapped power of creativity. When a writer abandons herself to its call, amazing things happen. On the surface the *cuento* of María Sabida may be interpreted as a parable of how a good woman conquers and tames a bad man. In the Spanish cultures, with their Holy Mother Mary mystique, the role of the woman as spiritual center and guide in a marriage is a central one. Men were born to sin; women, to redeem. But as a writer, I choose to interpret the tale of the woman who outmaneuvers the killer, who marries him so that she does not have to fear him, as a metaphor for the woman creator. The assassin is the destroyer of ambition, drive, and talent—the killer of dreams. It does not have to be a man. It is anything or anyone who keeps the artist from her work. The smartest woman on the island knows that she must trap the assassin so that he/she/it does not deprive her of her creative power. To marry the killer means to me that the artist has wedded the negative forces in her life that would keep her from fulfilling her mission and, furthermore, that she has made the negative forces work for her instead of against her.

Her sweetness is the vision of beauty that the artist carries within her, that few see unless she sacrifices herself. Does she have to be destroyed, or destroy herself so that the world can taste her sweet blood? Woolf, Plath, and Sexton may have thought so. I would rather believe that the sweetness may be shared without total annihilation, but not without pain or sacrifice: that is part of the formula for the honey-filled burlap sack that will save your life. The transaction that took place between María Sabida and her assassin-husband was a trade-off on macho. She took on his macho. He understood that. So they embraced. The artist and the world struck a compromise, albeit an uneasy one on her part. She had to sleep with one eye open and watch what was offered her to eat. Remember the sleep-inducing figs.

Some women eat sleep-inducing figs early in their lives. At first they are unwitting victims of this feminine appetizer. Later they reach for the plate. It is easier to sleep while life happens around you. Better to dream while others *do*. The writer recognizes the poisoned fruit. She may pretend to sleep and bear the pain of hot wax as she prepares herself for battle. But she knows what is happening around her at all times. And when she is ready, she will act. Occasionally my *comadre* will try to save other women who have eaten the *higos de sueño*. She will try to rouse them, to wake them up. And sometimes, the sleepers will rise and follow her to freedom. But very often, they choose to remain unconscious. They rise briefly, look around them. They see that the world goes on without them. They eat another fig and go back to sleep.

There is another kind of woman that my *comadre* cannot save: María La Loca, the woman who was left at the altar. I first heard my grandmother tell this *cuento* when I was a child in Puerto Rico. Later I wrote this poem:

The Woman Who Was Left at the Altar

She calls her shadow Juan,
looking back often as she walks.
She has grown fat, breasts huge
as reservoirs. She once opened her blouse
in church to show the silent town
what a plentiful mother she could be.
Since her old mother died, buried in black,
she lives alone. Out of the lace

she made curtains for her room,
doilies out of the veil. They are now
yellow as malaria.
She hangs live chickens from her waist to sell,
walks to the silent town swinging her skirts of flesh.
She doesn't speak to anyone. Dogs follow
the scent of blood to be shed. In their hungry,
yellow eyes she sees his face.
She takes him to the knife time after time.

Again this is a tale that is on the surface about the harsh lessons of love. But even my Mamá knew that it had a subtext. It was about failing oneself and blaming it on another. In my book *Silent Dancing,* I wrote around my Mamá's *cuento,* showing how she taught me about the power of storytelling through the tale of María La Loca. Mamá told it as a parable to teach her daughters how love can defeat you, if you are weak enough to let it.

There is a woman who comes to my *comadre* and complains that she knows that she has talent, that she has poetry in her, but that her life is too hard, too busy; her husband, her children are too demanding. She is a moral, responsible person and cannot in good conscience allow herself the luxury of practicing art. My *comadre* takes the time to tell this woman that she can choose to "learn to sleep with one eye open," to conjure up some female macho and claim the right to be an artist. But the woman is always prepared with an arsenal of reasons, all bigger than her needs, as to why she will die an unfulfilled woman, yearning to express herself in lyrical lines. She will, if pressed, imply that my *comadre* cannot possibly be a nurturing mother or caring partner, if she can find the time to write. In my culture, this type of woman who has perfected one art—that of self-abnegation, sometimes even martyrdom—is called *la sufrida,* the suffering one. There is much more admiration and respect for *la sufrida* in our society than there is for the artist.

The artist, too, suffers—but selfishly. She suffers mainly because the need to create torments her. If she is not fortunate enough to be truly selfish (or doesn't have enough macho in her to do as men have always done and claim the right, the time, and the space she needs), then she is doomed to do a balancing act, to walk the proverbial line that is drawn taut between the demands of her life—which may include choices that were made *before* she discovered her calling, such as marriage and children—and her art. The true artist will use her creativity to find a way, to carve the time, to claim a kitchen table, a library carrel, if a room of her own is not possible. She will use subterfuge if necessary, write poems in her recipe book, give up sleeping time or social time, and write.

Once I was asked to teach an evening writing class for a group of working-class Latinas who had taken the initiative to ask a community arts organization for a workshop they could attend. These women toiled at mind-numbing jobs eight or more hours each day, and most of them had several small children and a tired husband at home waiting for them to cook at the end of the workday. Yet somehow the women had found one another as artists. Perhaps on a lunch break one of them had dared to mention that she wrote poems or kept a journal. In any case, I met a determined group of tired women that first night, many nervously watching the clock because they had had to make complex arrangements to leave their homes on a weeknight. Perceiving that the needs of this class would be different from those of my usual writing students, I asked these women to write down their most pressing artistic problem. I read the slips of paper during the break and confirmed my intuition about them. Almost unanimously they had said that their main problem was no time and no place to write. When we came together again, I told them about my method of writing, how I had developed it because, by the time I knew I had to write, I was a young mother and wife and was teaching full-time. At the end of the day, after giving my child all of the attention I *wanted* to give her, grading papers, and doing the normal tasks involved with family life, I was done for. I could not summon a thought into my head, much less try to create. After trying various ways of finding time for myself, short of leaving everyone I loved behind for the sake of Art, I decided on the sacrifice I had to make—and there is always one: I had to give up some of my precious sleep time. In order to give myself what I needed, I had to stop eating the delicious sleep-inducing figs that also make you good at finding excuses for not becoming who you need to be. I started going to bed when my daughter did and rising at 5:00 A.M. And in the two hours before the household came alive and the demands on me began, I wrote and I wrote and I wrote. Actually, I usually had just enough time, after drinking coffee and bringing order to the chaos in my head, to write a few lines of a poem, or one or two pages on my novel—which took me, at that pace, three and one-half years to complete. But I was working, at a rate that many unencumbered writers would probably find laughably slow. But I wrote, and I write. And I am not left at the altar.

Each line that I lay on a page points me toward my *comadre* María Sabida and takes me farther away from falling into the role of *la sufrida*.

The first assignment I gave that group of women was this: to go home and create a place to write for themselves. It had to be a place that could be cordoned off somehow, a place where books and notes could be left without fear of someone disturbing them and ruining a thought left unfinished, and, also important, a place where no one would feel free to read a work in progress—to ridicule and perhaps inhibit the writer. Their second assignment: to come up with a plan to make time to write every day.

As I expected, this latter injunction caused an uproar. They each claimed that their situation was impossible: no room, no privacy, no time, no time, no time. But I remained firm. They were going to write their version of Virginia Woolf's "A Room of One's Own" to fit their individual lives.

Two evenings later I met them again. I recall the faces of those weary women on that night. They were tired but not beaten, as they were used to challenges and to dealing with nearly impossible odds. I had dared them to use the strength of character that allowed them to survive in a harsh world of barrio and factory and their endless *lucha*. The struggle for survival was familiar to them. One by one they read their *cuentos* of how they had made a writing corner for themselves, the most fortunate among them having a guest room that her mother-in-law often occupied. She turned it into her study and bought a lock; permission for other uses would have to be requested. Others had appropriated a corner here and there, set up a table and a chair, and screened off a space for themselves. The *No Trespassing* rules had been discussed with family members; even mild threats had been issued to nosy teenage children: You mess with my papers, I'll make free with your things. It was a celebration, minor declarations of independence by women used to yielding their private territory to others.

That night I saw that the act of claiming a bit of space and time for themselves was the beginning of something important for some of these women. Of course, not all of them would succeed against the thief of time. Some would find it easier to revert to the less fatiguing norm of the usual daily struggle. It takes a fierce devotion to defend your artistic space, and eternal vigilance over it, because the needs of others will grow like vines in your little plot and claim it back for the jungle. Finally, we came to the last writer in the circle. This was a young woman who always looked harried and disheveled in her old jeans and man's shirt. She had two sons, little hellions, both under six years of age, and an absent husband. The story she had brought to class the first night had made us cry and laugh. She had the gift, no doubt about it, but had been almost angry about the writing space and time assignment. She lived in a cramped apartment where the only table had to be used to store groceries, change babies, and iron. The story she had read to us had been written during a hospital stay. What was she to do, cut her wrists so that she could find time to write? We waited in respectful silence for her to begin reading. She surprised us by standing up and announcing that she had brought her writing place with her that night. Out of the back pocket of her jeans she pulled a handmade notebook. It had a sturdy cardboard covering, and within it was paper cut to fit and stitched together. There was also a small pencil that fit just right in the groove. She flipped the notebook open and began to read her essay. She had nearly given up trying to find a place to write. Everywhere she laid down her papers the kids had gotten to them. It became a game for them. At first she had been angry, but then she had decided to use her imagination to devise a way to write that was childproof. So she had come up with the idea of a portable room of her own. Because she could not leave her children and lock herself up in a room to write, she constructed a notebook that fit her jeans' pocket precisely. It had a hard back so that she could write on it while she went around the house or took the kids to the park, or even while grocery shopping. No one thought anything of it because it just looked like a housewife making a laundry list. She had even written this essay on her son's head while he leaned on her knees watching television.

Again there was laughter and tears. We had all learned a lesson that night about the will to create. I often think about this woman carrying her writing room with her wherever she went, and I have told her story often to other women who claim that the world keeps them from giving themselves to art. And I have put this young woman, who knew the meaning of *being* an artist, in my little pantheon of women who sleep with one eye open, the clapboard temple where I visit my storytelling *co-madre*, María Sabida, to seek her counsel.

There are no altars in this holy place, nor women who were left at one.

In Search of My Mentors' Gardens

A Fable for Our Times

Once upon a time a young girl lived in the house of English. The girl loved English, although English was not her mother tongue; she was her stepmother tongue. Mother English was both beautiful and cruel, and she preferred the company of men. Men used English in many ways, and English used them. She relished the action and the danger of men's lives. She is known to have partied with Beowulf's men, drinking strong spirits with them in their mead halls and staying up with them until the break of dawn making epic poems about their bloody conquests. She was seen with Chaucer at his table, middle age, eating greasy meat with her fingers. And, of course, we have all heard about the orgies she organized with Shakespeare, with whom she cavorted to near exhaustion.

Mother English rarely associated with women, and when she did she was feared for the damage she could, and often would, wreak on the delicate female brain and heart. It is said that English made certain women lose control and try to act like men. To love English as she demanded, a woman had to pay a high price, often surrendering her reputation, her sanity, and sometimes even her life. English was like a poisonous drug that corrupted a woman's mind and made her ignore her husband and children, for English took the place of men in women's hearts.

English's stepdaughter despaired when she discovered that her stepmother disdained not only women but also the foreign, the dark, the strange. The threat of spoiling her beauty by associating with mongrels sent English into a panic, and because her stepdaughter was not acceptable by her standards, being an ugly child acquired through a politically motivated union, she locked her up in a room whose original use she had forgotten. But the girl continued to love English because she had been brought to her house at a tender age and knew nothing and no one as well as she knew English.

It so happened that the room where the girl was imprisoned was also the place where English kept all her old paramours. The girl learned to love the men whom English had loved: Joyce, Lawrence, Byron, Shelley, Keats—there were so many proper and improper British gentlemen. Then later came the brash Americans who had taken English on wild rides: Hemingway, Fitzgerald, Faulkner. The girl studied the life of English through her affairs with these men and was entertained and educated by them; but still, she was lonely. She did not have any women in the room with her. No one of her own kind with whom to share and compare.

Many years passed before she came across a small secret shelf that contained the works of women who had made their pact with English: Woolf, Dickinson, Stein, Plath, Sexton. It was a great discovery because inside one of the books was the key that unlocked the door to the room.

When the girl emerged, she found the aging English playing solitaire, her mansion now occupied by strangers. She had apparently forgotten her stepdaughter because she invited her to a friendly game of cards. She seemed lonely and the girl felt pity for her.

"Why don't we join them instead? Who are they? They seem to be having a good time," she suggested, seeing that the place was full of people who acted as if they belonged in the house of English, speaking to one another in interesting new words she had not heard while locked up with English's old lovers.

"Stepchildren with their children, poor relatives, and other people they've brought here without my consent. They are loud, they talk fast, and I don't understand them," said Mother English.

"But they're speaking your language."

"No, they're not," insisted the old lady, but not with her old arrogance, rather with apparent fear.

The girl saw that English would need her help now that she was not the imperious woman she had been in earlier days. She offered her still beautiful stepmother her hand:

"Come on, Mother. Let's go introduce English to her new family. I'll help translate."

And Mother English, now too old and weary to resist, sighed in resignation, accepted her stepdaughter's hand, and joined the party.

THE END

Alice Walker on Flannery O'Connor:

As a college student in the sixties I read her books endlessly, scarcely conscious of the difference between her social and economic background and my own, but put them away in anger when I discovered that, while I was reading O'Connor—Southern, Catholic, and white—there were other women writers—some Southern, some religious, all black—I had not been allowed to know. For several years, while I searched for, found, and studied black women writers, I deliberately shut O'Connor out, feeling almost ashamed that she had reached me first. And yet, even when I no longer read her, I missed her, and realized that though the rest of America might not mind, having endured it so long, I would never be satisfied with a segregated literature. I would have to read Zora Hurston *and* Flannery O'Connor,

In Search of My Mentors' Gardens

Nella Larsen *and* Carson McCullers, Jean Toomer *and* William Faulkner, before I could feel well read at all.*

As a college student in the seventies' United States I had a similar realization: I needed to write and I had no models of my own kind. In fact I remember only one woman's name coming up for serious discussion in my classes and that was Virginia Woolf. Like the girl in my fable I was smitten with English literature but beginning to suspect that it was going to be an unrequited love. Unlike Alice Walker I had no indication that anyone out there was writing for me. My day of revelation arrived years later when I came across a book of stories written by someone whose gender I couldn't decide by the name alone. Flannery. What kind of person would have a name like that? After reading only one story—"Revelation"—I knew what kind of person, *my* kind. I had been living in the Deep South for several years by then, and trying to be politically correct and nonjudgmental about the strange idioms and customs of my neigh-

In Search of Our Mothers' Gardens: Womanist Prose, by Alice Walker (New York: Harcourt Brace and Co., 1983), 42–43.

bors (PC, that odious term, had not come into common usage at the time, so I believed I was trying to be polite to my hosts, a good Catholic girl amidst the passionate Protestants). But frankly, I was still baffled by the contradictions of the southern character. In my own ethnocentricity as a Catholic Puerto Rican woman living in the Bible Belt, I saw myself as part of the good minority group: my kind were generous and unbiased, tolerant and forbearing. Someday I was going to write poems and stories extolling these virtues of my people while exposing the Others for the oppressors they were.

"Revelation." O'Connor's stories left me as awestruck as Mrs. Turpin at the pig parlor. But I had a different vision from that of the nice, white, Christian lady who believes she knows exactly where she belongs in God's Great Scheme. In the waiting room of a doctor's office, which O'Connor brilliantly constructs as a microcosm of social classes in the South, Mrs. Turpin is struck by a book called *Human Development,* a missile directed at her by a college student whose ire she seems to have raised merely by being who she is. Mrs. Turpin is wounded spiritually by the girl's action as well as physically. She cannot understand why a nice, clean, hardworking lady like herself should be attacked so viciously by this plain girl who is and acts "ugly." The insult added to the injury is being called "you old warthog from hell." This incident leads Mrs. Turpin on a painful introspective journey into her soul of souls. By following the tortured path of her thinking, we learn that her system of values is based on division and classification. Of course she sets herself near the top of her Christian scale with others who have attained the American dream of having a little of everything safely, while she puts the black people at the bottom, with only the poor white trash in a lower slot. She is later shocked to realize not only that her carefully constructed chain of being is rejected by certain others, including the black people who work for her and who patronize her on cue, but also, and worse, that she has been judged and found morally lacking by those she considered her inferiors. During her visionary trance at the pig parlor, Mrs. Turpin's existential anguish leads her to a vision of eternal truth where her categories go topsy-turvy. From "Revelation":

There were whole companies of white-trash, clean for the first time in their lives, and bands of black niggers in white robes, and battalions of freaks and lunatics shouting and clapping and leaping like frogs. And bringing up the end of the procession was a tribe of people whom she recognized at once as those who, like herself and Claud, had always had a little of everything and the God-given wit to use it right. She leaned forward to observe them closer. They were marching behind the others with great dignity, accountable as they had always been for good order and common sense and respectable behavior. They alone were on key. Yet she could see by their shocked and altered faces that even their virtues were being burned away.

And so in one incomparable paragraph Flannery O'Connor sweeps up and away the social, economic, and racial hierarchies of her South and—although the term would not have been available for her to reject then—replaced political correctness with moral correctness. The levels still exist in the world but can be abolished in the heart and mind.

To O'Connor, a practicing Catholic, revelation was God's grace working through an individual. To me, it is another sort of epiphany. Most of us have a sense of ourselves as capable of moral choice and honesty. It is the same obligation of the artist to her art, to be honest, to share the insight, the vision. My revelation in reading O'Connor's "Revelation" was that I too was included in the motley crew she saw as part of Mrs. Turpin's vision. If I substitute the path leading toward heaven with the road toward inclusion in the only reality I know, that of my life here in this country among a diversity of people, then I too can count myself among the believers, perhaps even the saved.

What Alice Walker discovered, and to her great credit shared with her readers, is that O'Connor's art is encompassing of us all in its harsh and terrible beauty. Mrs. Turpin's revelation brings together all the personae of O'Connor's imagination modeled on the people she knew. Like the tough but fair God she believed in, she is equally brutal in her depiction of their foibles as well as gentle in their moments of grace. By using her equal-opportunity pen like a scalpel, which always made its incision shockingly close to the jugular, she gave us an unsentimental view of ourselves, made us think, offended us, and delighted us. In the end, when we have met, hated, recognized, and finally pitied the Mrs. Turpin in ourselves, we are both wounded and healed, made better by having gone under the knife.

Honesty as practiced by the writer is what I learned from O'Connor's art. The stories, poetry, and essays of Alice Walker taught me that a writer must never reject true art out of ego or self-righteousness, or for political reasons. Walker read and profited from O'Connor's stories that were written in the colloquial language of another time using what are now considered politically incorrect epithets. I wonder how the feisty Ms. O'Connor would have reacted to being told she could not use the *n* word in her work? Her books have been banned from some school libraries for their "racist" language. Yet this is how Alice Walker, one of the most important writers of our time, who also happens to be African American, assesses O'Connor's art. The occasion described in "Beyond the Peacock," an essay from *In Search of Our Mothers' Gardens,* is the end of a visit she and her mother made to Andalusia, the O'Connor farm in Milledgeville:

We walk about quietly, listening to the soft sweep of the peacocks' tails as they move across the yard. I notice how completely O'Connor, in her fiction, has described just this view of the rounded hills, the tree line, black against the sky, the dirt road that runs from the front yard down to the highway. I remind myself of her courage and of how much—in her art—she has helped me to see. She destroyed the last vestiges of sentimentality in white Southern writing; she caused white women to look ridiculous on pedestals, and she approached her black characters—as a mature artist—with unusual humility and restraint. She also cast spells and worked magic with the written word. The magic, the wit, and the mystery of Flannery O'Connor I know I will always love, I also know the meaning of the expression "Take what you can use and let the rest rot." If ever there was an expression designed to protect the health of the spirit, this is it.

Years after Flannery O'Connor's stories revealed to me that I wanted to be her kind of writer, at least as honest, I encountered Alice Walker's healthy spirit in action in a story that, along with "Revelation," has taught me the power of truth in writing. This is the way the narrator describes herself in "Everyday Use," a story about intellectual hubris and the need to value art for its function in our daily lives.

I am a large, big-boned woman with rough, man-working hands. In the winter I wear flannel nightgowns to bed and overalls during the day. I can kill and clean a hog as mercilessly as a man. My fat keeps me hot in zero weather. I can work outside all day, breaking ice to get water for washing; I can eat pork liver cooked over the open fire minutes after it comes steaming from the hog. One winter I knocked a bull calf straight in the brain between the eyes with a sledge hammer and had the meat up to chill before nightfall.

No woman on a pedestal there. No easy sentimentality. Just the truth.

"Everyday Use" is about a college educated woman who comes home to her mother's house in rural Georgia to claim a family quilt as well as other heirlooms that she wants to display as artifacts. Walker's incisive depiction of the girl who has adopted all the trappings of the progressive black intellectual in the sixties (has even changed her traditional, family name, Dee, to a preposterous-sounding African name, Wangero) and realistic portrayal of the strong mother and the fire-scarred, timid sister are lessons in making art that transcends social, political, and racial boundaries. The fact that they are black women is important — race is a crucial element of the story — but the knowledge we gain is universal, at the level of what O'Connor called "the eternal truth." The characters' lives concern us all. In Walker's story, the main symbol of the misuse of history, culture, and art is the family quilt. The sister Maggie and the mother understand the true value of the quilt. It was made out of the pieces of real lives by women related to them by blood and tradition for the everyday use of their loved ones. Walker like O'Connor rejects the intellectualization of art, its appropriation by outsiders who may have little or no understanding of its original intended true function: to comfort, to heal, to connect, and to share a vision. The vision belongs to the tribe. And that vision may be given to the least rather than to the greatest.

In "Everyday Use" the mother makes a decision about the quilts that one daughter covets and the other daughter needs:

When I looked at her like that something hit me in the top of my head and ran down the soles of my feet. Just like when I'm in church and the spirit of God touches me and I get happy and shout. I did something I never had done before: hugged Maggie to me, then dragged her on into the room, snatched the quilts out of Miss Wangero's hands and dumped them into Maggie's lap. Maggie just sat there on my bed with her mouth open.

The quilts are thus put to their rightful use.

Rightful use is what I look for in my life and in my art. I want my stories, poems, and essays to be put to everyday use. I don't want them to be simply tokens of culture and race, or to become artifacts of my particular time in history. I would like some powerful person to dump my words on someone's lap to be used as needed.

Flannery O'Connor once told about giving some of her stories to a neighbor in Milledgeville:

and when she returned them, she said, "Well, them stories just gone and shown you how some folks *would* do," and I thought to myself that that was right; when you write stories, you have to be content to start exactly there—showing how some specific folks *will* do, *will* do in spite of everything.

These two writers, who have revealed so much to me, shared with me a belief that human nature is more complex than black and white; and they wrote about both what they saw reflected in their own mirrors and what they observed happening out their windows. Their hope, and mine as their apprentice, is that the reader might also catch a glimpse of herself when she looks into that glass darkly. We can get her to look by our prompting. Preferably by polite prompting, but sometimes we may have to hit her over the head.

And Are You a Latina Writer?

Back in 1978, having just finished graduate school and feeling somewhat inhibited by having read and dissected the major works of great, dead men of letters, I thought I'd be glad if someday someone referred to me simply as a "writer." Now I find myself not just a writer, but bearing the added responsibility of being a *Latina* writer. What is a Latina writer, and how did I become one? My case as a developing Latina writer is somewhat different from others in that, except for the years during my childhood when my family lived in Puerto Rico and in a Puerto Rican neighborhood in Paterson, New Jersey, I have lived in relative geographical isolation from the Latino communities of the United States.

I stress the word *geographical* because, in my mind, I have never abandoned the island of my birth, or perhaps that obsession called "the Island" has never left me. It is the subject of much of my writing. However, I am not a scholar in the field of Latino literature, but rather a writer of books written in English whose main subjects and settings often reflect the author's emigrant background and issues pertaining to her ethnicity. I would like to reiterate some of the questions that have been put to me by persons trying to determine whether I am a Puerto Rican writer:

Why don't you write in Spanish? Isn't writing in English a selling out to the mainstream culture on your part?

My choice of languages is not a political statement: English is my literary language, the language I learned in the schools of the country where my parents brought me to live as a child. Spanish is my familial language, the tongue I speak with my blood relatives, that I dream in, that lies between the lines of my English sentences. The Puerto Rican American writer, Nicholasa Mohr, summed it up best when she stated in an essay about her work, "Because I am a daughter of the Puerto Rican Diaspora, English is the language that gives life to my work, the characters I create, and that stimulates me as a writer." *

* "Puerto Rican Writers in the U.S., Puerto Rican Writers in Puerto Rico: A Separation Beyond Language," in *Breaking Boundaries: Latina Writing and*

And Are You a Latina Writer?

Isn't the barrio what you write about? Don't you need a sense of place and community for your art? What are you doing in Georgia?

These are the questions I am often asked by people who cannot imagine what a *puertorriqueña* is doing in the Deep South. Once I heard that a Puerto Rican writer had asked where I lived; on hearing the answer, she had said, "No wonder she's mad." At first, offended, I took that "mad" to mean "crazy," but I decided that a benevolent interpretation would be better: What my colleague had obviously meant was that my isolation from others like her, like myself by extension, had not prevented me from being a part of what Las Vasquez has referred to as the phenomenon of the Latina as "the angry storyteller." I choose to believe that my fellow writer, my *compañera* in art, meant that living in the piney woods has not dissipated the passion of my art. Because my literary universe exists within me, and although admitting the need for "community" where the free exchange of ideas can be stimulating, I write in isolation and anywhere that I can find a room of my own.

Critical Readings, edited by Asunsion Horno-Delgado, Eliana Ortega, Nina M. Scott, and Nancy Saporta Sternback (Amherst: University of Massachusetts Press, 1989), 12.

In the isolation of my art I find a significant relation to the separateness that is an inherent component of my psyche as the child of emigrants. In his Nobel lecture, Octavio Paz spoke of "this consciousness of being separate [as a] constant feature of our [Latino] spiritual history." He also proposed that our divided souls may be the genesis for our most powerful artistic expression: "[Our isolation creates] an anguished awareness that invites self-examination, at other times it appears as a challenge, a spur to action, to go forth and encounter others and the outside world." His conclusion is that, although he speaks as a Mexican writer, out of his particular experiences and worldview, aloneness is the condition of humankind, and as artists our goal is to build the bridges "to overcome the separation and reunite us with the world and our fellow beings."

In the 1960s, growing up in two confusing and increasingly fragmented cultures, I absorbed literature, both the spoken *cuentos* I heard the women in my family tell and the books I buried my head in as if I were a creature who consumed paper and ink for sustenance. As a young college student I first majored in sociology, hoping to find a way to change the world. With the Vietnam War on my TV screen daily and the other ongoing attacks on my political naïveté, it was not long before the spell of innocence was broken. For the spiritual sustenance I craved I returned to my first love, literature. Although the world was tearing itself asunder, each author I read put it back together for me, giving order to chaos, however fleetingly. While I was visiting the realm of its creator, the poem, the story, or the novel made sense of things for me. I decided that words were my medium; language could be tamed. I could make it perform for me, if I could only hold back the madness outside with my pen. In other words, I had to believe that my work was important to my being. My mission as an emerging writer became to use my art as a bridge, so that I would not be like my parents, who precariously straddled cultures, always fearing the fall, anxious as to which side they really belonged to; I would be crossing the bridge of my design and construction, at will, not abandoning either side, but traveling back and forth without fear and confusion as to where I belonged—I belong to both.

This is what it means to me to be a Puerto Rican American writer: to claim my heritage—to drink from the life-giving waters of my own backyard well, to eat the mango fruit of knowledge of good and evil that grows in Borinquen, the tropical island of my grandmother's tales, as well as to acknowledge the troubled, real country of Puerto Rico I can travel back to any time I desire—and also to claim the language of my education, English, the culture and literature of the country I was brought to as a child. I claim both. I plant my little writer's flag on both shores. There are exclusivists who would have me choose sides: I do not find such a choice necessary, any more than Isaac Bashevis Singer gave up being Jewish when he wrote his universal tales, any more than Alice Walker denies her African American roots and Deep South beginnings to write her American novels. It is neither necessary nor beneficial to me as a writer and an individual to give up anything that makes me a whole person.

Where does your work belong in the American literature canon?

I am glad to have to consider this question at all. I feel that I risk hubris in addressing it. I believe that the work of Latina writers, myself included, belongs, if it is judged worthy enough, alongside the work of other American writers whose work reflects the concerns of people experiencing our time. There common ground is found, at the level of our obsessions. In an important essay that defines Latina writing, the editors of *Breaking Boundaries: Latina Writings and Critical Readings* have stated, "the Latina writer will often prioritize the lives of women who have, like themselves, carved an existence within a woman's space. More specifically, their recognition and celebration of what we call 'a matriarchal heritage' can be expressed in remarks such as Ana Castillo's: 'We all have our *abuelita* (little grandmother) poems.' It is not infrequent in Latina discourse to pay tribute to a long line of female ancestors" (12).

I had no idea when I wrote the following early poem about my grandmother that I was falling into the category of Latina writer. The only major woman writer I had heard "speak" directly to me from the canon I was following in graduate school was Virginia Woolf, and it would be many years later that I would read her "A Room of One's Own" in which she stated: "A Woman Writing thinks back through her mothers."

Claims

Last time I saw her, Grandmother
had grown seamed as a Bedouin tent.
She had claimed the right
to sleep alone, to own

her nights, to never bear
the weight of sex again, nor to accept
its gift of comfort, for the luxury
of stretching her bones.
She'd carried eight children,
three had sunk in her belly, *náufragos,*
she'd called them, shipwrecked babies
drowned in her black waters.
Children are made in the night and
steal your days
for the rest of your life, amen. She said this
to each of her daughters in turn.
Once she had made a pact with man and nature
and kept it. Now like the sea
she is claiming back her territory.

Since then I have thought back through my mothers through
dozens of poems, essays, short stories, and a novel. And not just
my mothers through biology, but also my literary mothers
who include a wealthy Victorian called Woolf; several African
American matriarchs such as Mother Morrison and Sisters
Walker and Dove; my southern muses, greatest among them
Flannery O'Connor; the cousins from South and Central Amer-

ica, Allende and Esquivel; my closest contemporary Puerto Rican kin-through-art from my own Island and the U.S.; and the work of my contemporary Latina writers whose example inspires and encourages me. My mothers are all strong women, but they are not all *puertorriqueñas.*

Finally, I am not lost in America. I am not searching for an identity. I know who I am and what I am. And although community is nice for a writer to have—a group to discuss work in progress with, a cafe to socialize with others who share her interests—I do not believe those things are necessary to the production of a work. In my case, specifically, I don't feel a need to have others authenticate my work as "Puerto Rican" literature.

Although I often seek the counsel of my scholarly colleagues who are experts in the field of Puerto Rican literature and culture—which I'm not, and I freely and gratefully accept their assistance and expertise—I do my best work in a room alone. I am not confused about my cultural identity. I know what I am because my *puertorricanness* was not awarded to me: it is part of me; it cannot be legislated out. It can be said and it can be written that one is or is not a Puerto Rican writer, but one's essence cannot be either given or taken away. Whether I write in Spanish or English, I am who I am: a writer who is a Puerto Rican woman, whether I live in New York City or on a farm in Georgia.

Because I am vigilant about keeping my work free from the constraints of external interference, the push for political and other agendas, I have an even greater need to get back to what Octavio Paz described as "that time I wrote without wondering why I was doing it."

In my books I follow memories, *cuentos,* events, and characters that I see as my guides back to what Virginia Woolf calls "moments of being" in my life, both in Puerto Rico and in the United States. It is a process of discovery. My books are neither Puerto Rican emigrant history nor sociological case studies; at least, I didn't write them as such. I tell stories that recount the suffering and joy of the Puerto Rican emigrants of my experience, mainly women; I re-envision the scenes of my youth and transform them through my imagination, attempting to synthesize the collective yearnings of these souls into a collage that means Puerto Rican to me, that gives shape to my individual vision. If these *cuentos* I create out of my memory and imbue with my perceptions add up to a universal message, then

I consider myself fortunate to have accomplished much more than I allow myself to hope for when I sit down in front of that blank sheet of paper that calls to my restless spirit like a believer's candle. No longer the idealistic young poet hoping to find big answers to big questions, I am content now to be the solitary traveler, the *caminante:* my main hope—to find a pattern in the trees, the path less traveled by in the woods. I know to whom these woods belong: if I'm lucky I will find her *casa* in the clearing, always just ahead of me—my little-old-lady muse, my *abuela,* sitting in her rocking chair waiting to tell me another *cuento;* through her storytelling, she teaches me the way back home.

And May He Be Bilingual

Latin Women Pray

Latin women pray

In incense sweet churches

They pray in Spanish

To an Anglo God

With a Jewish heritage.

And this Great White Father

Imperturbable

In his marble pedestal

Looks down upon

His brown daughters

Votive candles shining like lust

In his all seeing eyes

Unmoved

By their persistent prayers.

And May He Be Bilingual

Yet year after year
Before his image they kneel
Margarita, Josefina, Maria, and Isabel
All fervently hoping
That if not omnipotent
At least He be bilingual.

In this early poem I express the sense of powerlessness I felt as a non-native speaker of English in the United States. Non-native. Non-participant in the mainstream culture. *Non,* as in no, not, nothing. This little poem is about the non-ness of the non-speakers of the ruling language making a pilgrimage to the only One who can help, hopeful in their faith that someone is listening, yet still suspicious that even He doesn't understand their language. I grew up in the tight little world of the Puerto Rican community in Paterson, New Jersey, and later moved to Augusta, Georgia, where my "native" universe shrank even further to a tiny group of us who were brought to the Deep South through the military channels our fathers had chosen out of economic necessity. I wrote this ironic poem years ago, out of a need to explore the loneliness, the almost hopelessness, I had felt and observed in the other non-native speakers, many my own relatives, who would never master the English language well enough to be able to connect with the native speakers in as significant ways as I did.

Having come to age within the boundaries of language exiles, and making only brief forays out into the vast and often frightening landscape called *the mainstream,* it's easy for the newcomer to become ethnocentric. That's what Little Italy, Little Korea, Little Havana, Chinatown, and barrios are, centers of ethnic concerns. After all, it's a natural human response to believe that there is safety only within the walls around the circle of others who look like us, speak like us, behave like us: it is the animal kingdom's basic rule of survival—if whatever is coming toward you does not look like you or your kin, either fight or fly.

It is this primal fear of the unfamiliar that I have conquered through education, travel, and my art. I am an English teacher by profession and a writer by vocation. I have written several books of prose and poetry based mainly on my experiences in growing up Latina in the United States. Until a few years ago, when multiculturalism became part of the American political agenda, no one seemed to notice my work; suddenly I find myself a Puerto Rican/American (Latina)/Woman writer. Not only am I supposed to share my particular vision of American life, but I am also supposed to be a role model for a new generation of Latino students who expect me to teach them how to get a piece of the proverbial English language pie. I actually enjoy both of these public roles, in moderation. I love teaching literature. Not my own work, but the work of my literary ancestors in English and American literature—my field, that is, the main source of my models as a writer. I also like going into my classrooms at the University of Georgia, where my English classes at this point are still composed mainly of white American students, with a sprinkling of African American and Asian American, and only occasionally a Latino, and sharing my bicultural, bilingual views with them. It is a fresh audience. I am not always speaking to converts.

I teach American literature as an outsider in love with the Word—whatever language it is written in. They, at least some of them, come to understand that my main criterion when I teach is excellence and that I will talk to them about so-called minority writers whom I admire in the same terms as I will the old standards they know they are supposed to honor and study. I show them why they should admire them, not blindly, but with a critical eye. I speak English with my Spanish accent to these native speakers. I tell them about my passion for the genius of humankind, demonstrated through literature: the power of language to affect, to enrich, or to diminish and destroy lives, its potential to empower someone like me, someone like them. The fact that English is my second language does not seem to matter beyond the first few lectures, when the students sometimes look askance at one another, perhaps wondering whether they have walked into the wrong classroom and at any moment this obviously "Spanish" professor will ask them to start conjugating regular and irregular verbs. They can't possibly know this about me: in my classes, everyone is safe from Spanish grammar recitation. Because almost all of my formal education has been in English, I avoid all possible risk of falling into a discussion of the uses of the conditional or of the merits of the subjunctive tense in the Spanish language: Hey, I just *do* Spanish, I don't explain it.

Likewise, when I *do* use my Spanish and allude to my Puerto Rican heritage, it comes from deep inside me where my imagination and memory reside, and I do it through my writing. My poetry, my stories, and my essays concern themselves with the coalescing of languages and cultures into a vision that has meaning first of all for me; then, if I am served well by my craft and the transformation occurs, it will also have meaning for others as art.

My life as a child and teenager was one of constant dislocation. My father was in the U.S. Navy, and we moved back to Puerto Rico during his long tours of duty abroad. On the Island, my brother and I attended a Catholic school run by American nuns. Then it was back to Paterson, New Jersey, to try to catch up, and sometimes we did, academically, but socially it was a different story altogether. We were the perennial new kids on the block. Yet when I write about these gypsy days, I construct a continuity that allows me to see my life as equal to any other, with its share of chaos, with its own system of order. This is what I have learned from writing as a minority person in America that I can teach my students: Literature is the human search for meaning. It is as simple and as profound as that. And we are all, if we are thinking people, involved in the process. It is both a privilege and a burden.

Although as a child I often felt resentful of my rootlessness, deprived of a stable home, lasting friendships, the security of one house, one country, I now realize that these same circumstances taught me some skills that I use today to adapt in a constantly changing world, a place where you can remain in one spot for years and still wake up every day to strangeness wrought by technology and politics. We can stand still and find ourselves in a different nation created overnight by decisions we did not participate in making. I submit that we are all becoming more like the immigrant and can learn from her experiences as a stranger in a strange land. I know I am a survivor in language. I learned early that possessing the secret of words was to be my passport into mainstream life. Notice I did not say "assimilation" into mainstream life. This is a word that has come to mean the acceptance of loss of native culture. Although I know for a fact that to survive everyone "assimilates" what they need out of many different cultures, especially in America, I prefer to use the term "adapt" instead. Just as I acquired the skills to adapt to American life, I have now come to terms with a high-tech world. It is not that different. I learned English to communicate, but now I know computer language. I have been greedy in my grasping and hoarding of words. I own enough stock in English to feel secure in almost any situation where my language skills have to serve me; and I have claimed my rich Puerto Rican culture to give scope and depth to my personal search for meaning.

As I travel around this country I am constantly surprised by the diversity of its peoples and cultures. It is like a huge, colorful puzzle. And the beauty is in its complexity. Yet there are some things that transcend the obvious differences: great literature, great ideas, and great idealists, for example. I find Don Quixote plays almost universal; after all, who among us does not have an Impossible Dream? Shakespeare's wisdom is planetary in its appeal; Ghandi's and King's message is basic to the survival of our civilization, and most people know it; and other voices that are like a human racial memory speak in a language that can almost always be translated into meaning.

And genius doesn't come in only one package: The Bard happened to be a white gentleman from England, but what about our timid Emily Dickinson? Would we call on her in our class, that mousy little girl in the back of the room squinting at the chalkboard and blushing at everything? We almost lost her art to neglect. Thank God poetry is stronger than time and prejudices.

This is where my idealism as a teacher kicks in: I ask myself, who is to say that at this very moment there isn't a Native American teenager gazing dreamily at the desert outside her window as she works on today's assignment, seeing the universe in a grain of sand, preparing herself to share her unique vision with the world. It may all depend on the next words she hears, which may come out of my mouth, or yours. And what about the African American boy in a rural high school in Georgia who showed me he could rhyme for as long as I let him talk. His teachers had not been able to get him to respond to literature. Now they listened in respectful silence while he composed an ode to his girl and his car extemporaneously, in a form so tight and so right (contagious too) that when we discuss the exalted Alexander Pope's oeuvre, we call it heroic couplets. But he was intimidated by the manner in which Pope and his worthy comrades in the canon had been presented to him and his classmates, as gods from Mt. Olympus, inimitable and incomprehensible to mere mortals like himself. He was in turn surprised to see, when it was finally brought to his attention, that Alexander Pope and he shared a good ear.

What I'm trying to say is that the phenomenon we call culture in a society is organic, not manufactured. It grows where we plant it. Culture is our garden, and we may neglect it, trample on it, or we may choose to cultivate it. In America we are dealing with varieties we have imported, grafted, cross-pollinated. I can only hope the experts who say that the land is replenished in this way are right. It is the ongoing American experiment, and it has to take root in the classroom first. If it doesn't succeed, then we will be back to praying and hoping that at least He be bilingual.

To Understand *El Azul*

We dream in the language we all understand,
in the tongue that preceded alphabet and word.
Each time we claim beauty from the world,
we approximate its secret grammar, its silent
syntax; draw nearer to the Rosetta stone
for dismantling Babel.

If I say *el azul,* you may not see the color
of *mi cielo, mi mar.* Look once upon my sky,
my sea, and you will know precisely
what *el azul* means to me.

Begin with this: the cool kiss
of a September morning in Georgia, the bell-shaped
currents of air changing in the sky, the sad ghosts
of smoke clinging to a cleared field, and the way

To Understand *El Azul*

days will taste different in your mouth each week
of the season. *Sábado:* Saturday
is strawberry. *Martes:* Tuesday
is bitter chocolate to me.

Do you know what I mean?

Still, everything we dream circles back.
Imagine the bird who returns home every night
with news of a miraculous world just beyond
your private horizon. To understand its message
first you must decipher its dialect of distance,
its idiom of dance. Look for clues
in its arching descent; in the way it resists
gravity. Above all, you have to learn why
it aims each day

toward the boundless *azul.*